Charlotte!

You're Going to Walk

Thank you for your help in my journey!

God Bless You

My Memoir

Laurie Perlongo Zappulla

You're Going to Walk

By Laurie Perlongo Zappulla

Available from Amazon.Com, CreateSpace.Com, and other retail outlets. Printed in the United States of America.

ISBN 13: 978-1724158680

TABLE OF CONTENTS

DEDICATION

I am proud and humbled to dedicate this story to my fellow Spinal Cord Injured community. My fellow people who endure this life that is difficult. And to the many others who are struggling with an incurable illness or a difficult injury. I hope that you find my stories relatable, compassionate and humble. Sensitive and filled with hope and encouragement.

My journey in all of this has been full of many emotions. I learned to adjust to those. I learned to keep believing against all hope. I learned that in my difficulties, I struggled at first, but I let my heart be mended. It was healed and is still being healed by the power of love.

I wrote a song many years ago, when I was ready to let faith guide me. It led me to "making all things new."

I heard it said, "When you can tell your story, when you can tell your struggle without shedding a tear, then you are healed."

ACKNOWLEDGEMENTS

My heart is filled with so much gratitude; I am blessed by so many special people:

The Editors- Eda Dichter, Tom Bowers, Potomac Green Writers Group, Jan Walker

Design and Technical thanks to:

Becky Johnson- Graphic Designer- book cover

Saul-Sjs Foto- photographer

Jordan Zappulla- photographer

Pat & Ed Smith- technical

♡ Always indebted and grateful for ♡

Donna Twist Ph.D. – I used to say that you were *The Best*. Always, always forever grateful for your belief in hope. Your belief in me. Your courage to say those very words that began my journey. Your words were jewels. I am indebted and blessed.

Tamar Martin Ph.D. – You believed in me, and still do. You make it easy to believe in myself. Your encouragement and honesty are everything. Thank you!

Dr. Brian Subach, Neurosurgeon – You were confident and that made us feel confident. We knew from the first time that we met you that you would be the only surgeon to repair my neck. Thank you, thank you.

Viraj Chang MPT/CPI- I told you that I may be your most challenging client. You didn't hesitate to see possibilities. Your continued guidance and care is outstanding. Your my master teacher and motivate me to be the best that I could be.

In memory of: Rev. D. Mercaldo- You're probably smiling in heaven; your faith brought healing to me so that I may share it to others.

All the prayers!!!!!! I do mean to everyone who has ever prayed for me and who continue to pray for me. I am so grateful for your love.

Rev. Patrick Mahoney, Director of Christian Defense Coalition & Church on the Hill- Your prayers during this process was such a blessing!

My Florida family!

To My family

Mom- You gave me so much. I am so grateful for your steadfast love. I am forever your beautiful girl and you are forever my beautiful Mother.

My brothers Rich & Vin and their families: So much love and support. From the very beginning we stayed united in believing that I would overcome this. You are my cheerleaders. My family to the moon!

My extended family- Paul's family, has always been supporting and loving, I love you back!

And *my* FAMILY- My husband Paul, my love. Jordan, my heart and gift. Your love and patience with me through this has been my steady. You never doubted; and you believed in me.

INSPIRATION

She said to me, "In a dream, I saw God tear out pages from his book of life and send them to you so that you can give life…

A stranger.

"Remember that you asked me, if you should compare yourself to disabled individuals or normal. I said, You're better than normal. You surpass normal because you endure normal life normally while being disabled. Therefore, you are better than normal. Makes sense to me."

A great friend.

INTRODUCTION

All this time. Ever since the beginning, people would say to me, "Wow, you should write a book." They would engage me with questions about what happened. They wanted to know, and they still do. So, BECAUSE SOMEONE WILL ALWAYS ASK…I began one night to write this story that I have known so well for the last 39 years. They say *that everyone has a book in them. They have a story to tell.* I never dreamed that my life story would be able to give hope to someone else. I knew it was amazing that I came back from a horrific injury, and thought it ended there. I have been wrong. People find it inspiring. They say, "that someone needs to hear this."

CHAPTER ONE

The ridiculous, unpleasant, painful, and nasty part is that I knew instantly. I'm paralyzed, my body just shut down, and my head and neck are vibrating, all the way down the spine, like the coils of a cheap massage device. I just hit my head on the bottom of a swimming pool.

All of this is happening in nanoseconds. I am drowning. My thoughts are rapid, in beat with my heart and I can hear my body, desperate to breathe and understand. I am tumbling around at the pool bottom, it is dark, and I am spinning. Finally, I am able to look towards the sky or upward. I see my cousin; she is on the ladder waiting to jump herself. Then I hear my name, my first and last name, this is official. I know it is God, somehow, I know. I hear a voice say, "Laurie Perlongo, if you do not come up, you will not come back."

I don't have to wonder if I am paralyzed. It is consuming me. The collision with the pool bottom, the trauma to the spine and spinal cord, the exact time that all this is happening, technically, my body ceased. My spinal cord is damaged badly. My head and neck are heavy, and they are pounding; I am thinking that I am going to die; I am trying to wake up from this nightmare. *This really can't be happening, not now,* I kept thinking. I'm trying to fix it. I am trying to put my feet on the bottom of the pool; they must be touching it, I just couldn't tell. I quickly realize they are unable to move in any sense; or able to get me out of this situation. My body is in a strange place, an unknown; because even if I explain it a thousand times, I will fail at making you understand its totality. Everything inside my body is internally humming; tuning fork like tremors. Yet, it also seemed to have "left the building." Some people like to think it is the same as when your leg or arm goes numb. "Oh, it's that tingling sort of thing, or like when you hit your funny bone" people say when they want to *relate.* Well, no, it so much more than that. There isn't anything funny about it.

1

The knowing – that you could die at this very moment – puts you in the *do or die* mode. *There is no tomorrow,* or *later. It is now or never.* All these clichés must have been written by someone with a similar death experience, a trauma so fast and shocking, that these desperate moments for another chance to live, are all you can see, feel or think in the moment. Suddenly, it felt as if I was pushed above the water line, I think by angels, one on each elbow, just high enough, so I can say "help." It is then that those incredible *God-showups* which is what I call them, began.

So, what does one *see* when people who are close to death say, "I saw my whole life flash before me, in this moment"?

I did not see my whole life. As in seeing scenes chronologically from my childhood to present? No, my version was edited. I saw two scenes from the movie that I had seen only two days before this accident. In "The Other Side of the Mountain," the newly paralyzed Olympic hopeful had a bad fall in the downhill skiing trials. She was instantly paralyzed, and she became a high-quadriplegic, meaning above the C5 vertebra, and not able to move anything. In therapy, she was strapped onto a straight wooden board. Purposely and suddenly, she was flipped over, and the flip made a loud noise. Like the crack of a whip, or the snap of the reality that she was facing.

The harsh flip into the unknown, the flip into "this is how life is now." *This sucks* and many other dark impressions pressed into my brain with the same snap! The second scene that I "saw" was when the skier was so excited, after months of rehab, that she could pick up a potato chip from a dish. It was a big achievement for her, but it only fed her fiancé's disappointed hopes of her ever walking again. All this is in my brain at the exact moment that I am drowning? How could this be?

In my own version of that movie, I've played that scene over and over in my head countless times, to try and make sense of this. I saw both the darkness of the pool bottom and the light above. I was flipped around, a few times tumbling, all in this fleeting time. Or at least it felt like that. Time stopped and so did I. It was as if this suspended time—this valley of the shadow of death—when I saw the sunlight above the water line and knew that it was where I had to be, I did not want to drown!

But wait, how odd is it that I would see this movie only two days before I would break my own neck? I had just seen this movie with the same cousin who was with me in the pool. I remember that we cried a lot, it was so sad. I had never even heard of anyone or known anyone who was quadriplegic. I understood quad, meaning four, but the *plegic* part? It means cessation of motion. That afternoon we did jumps and flips into the pool just like we had so many times before. I'm still trying to understand it all, but sometimes it hurts too much, and just *dealing* takes all of your time. Like Carly Simon sings, "I haven't got time for the pain. Have to learn how to leave myself behind, how to turn down the noise in my mind."

SEVEN HUNDRED STRANGERS

"Help!!" was the scream that the off-duty police officer heard when he was in his own pool that afternoon. His schedule had been changed just the day before. He told my uncle weeks later that earlier that morning, he had gotten a phone call from his captain to ask if he would switch his schedule. He was supposed to work that afternoon. He figured he would catch up on yard work and then go for a swim. When he heard the cry for help, he jumped over several fences to get to me. As he entered the pool, he knew to put me in a chaise lounge and float me. The initial seconds or minutes after the injury is so important. Sadly, additional damage has been done to SCI (spinal-cord injury) people because they were picked up or grabbed wrong; which can cause further damage if they aren't handled correctly. This police officer knew exactly what to do with me, in this fragile condition. He kept me floating until the ambulance came.

The second *God-show up* was that of our cousin, who is an ob-gyn specialist. Working at the hospital on that holiday weekend, she was having coffee with the best neurosurgeon on Staten Island when the ambulance driver wanted to verify if she really was a doctor, let alone my actual cousin. She answered the call and confirmed. Then she turned and said to Doctor Leventhal, "I need you, it's family." This one still boggles my mind. I mean what are the chances that on the last summer holiday weekend, my cousin and this neuro would be at the hospital working, let alone in the doctors' lounge when the phone call came through.

The next *God-show up* was my uncle's neighbor. Her name was Carol, and she had known me as a young girl, who came to visit on holidays and summer vacations. Carol was a born-again, a what? Some strange Catholic? She went the very next night to the Wednesday service of her Christian non-denominational church. It was Gateway Church, and 700 people there prayed for a young girl, they prayed for her neighbors' niece, she's paralyzed, she is only eighteen.

And there were some other *God-showups* in between. That's what I called all those odd times when miraculous things happened, and it was not just coincidence. Timing and provision were just right and unexplainable. Logic and science did not make sense, that's when faith takes over. If you're not a person of faith, you may call them coincidences, but I call them God's intervention, he showed up and things happened.

I remember thinking, "Oh man, this is big time, I am in big trouble!" When the E.M.T. strapped my head into the neck brace and pulled the other straps across my lower body, I was on a wooden board, on the gurney. The ambulance ride was horrible. All the noise that's happening in the background; the radio in the ambulance, the typical walkie-talkie static conversations with a pause in between. The other two technicians speaking to each other in medical terms, while one was hooking me up to IV and checking my heart rate—It's all so overwhelming! I remember screaming to the emergency tech, "I can't feel anything! I can't feel!" That poor guy—he was young, but he was confident. He kept trying to comfort me as best he could. He held my hand and assured me that I would be okay, but I could see on his face that he was being professional and what he really wanted to say was, "I am sorry, I am so sorry."

I WAS ONLY EIGHTEEN

"Stop worrying about your brand-new bathing suit. You have a lot more to freaking worry about," my cousin the doctor was telling me in my ear as I was rushed into St. Vincent's emergency room in Staten Island, N.Y. It was busy, there were many doctors and nurses coming in and out of the space where they put me. It felt like I was put in the lobby for display, because it seemed that every doctor working that day came by to see me. I became horrified because of all the seriousness. I want to scream, "Hey, what is going on! This was huge, I am in such big freaking trouble."

Just a few hours earlier that day, life was all an adventure. I had a few days to enjoy before I ventured back into the city to attend my first semester at some fancy, swanky fashion college in New York City. The 1979 fall semester was just starting, and I was ready to become the next buyer for some big fashion house – more like sweep the floors for some cranky designer – but who cared? I was eighteen!

"You have suffered a cervical fracture. Your sixth cervical vertebra is incompletely fractured, you are an incomplete quadriplegic, or, yes, your neck is broken. Can you squeeze my hand, can you wiggle your toes?" The E.R. doctor welcomed me with that statement and those very two questions that I would hear for the next few months.

They also kept asking me, "Where is your mother"? After the exhausting ambulance ride and getting into a room, the rest is just a blur. I could not respond because of all the drugs they gave me and the severe exhaustion of my mind that was screaming angry thoughts. I was screaming loudly, but they kept shushing me. They continued asking me, "Where did she travel to?" Well, she is only on her lifelong dream trip to seven different European cities and countries! Mom even said to me before she left, "Don't call me, I'll be back, and even if you break your arm, the travel agent's card is where my bills are, but try not to call her! Call your uncle!" Imagine, I was the only one who knew how to contact her through that white business card with a red globe on it! For a few hours, I was awake for a few seconds, and then fell back into a coma-like, morphine-induced sleep; and time was passing, they wanted to get me into surgery. Finally, I remembered, I had to tell my uncle; this was great timing, the doctors were all prepared to repair my neck, not make me walk, just repair it just so I could sit up—in a wheelchair, forever.

HEAVY METAL IN MY FUTURE

They called for the "C." Immediately, I was put into a cervical thongs device at St. Vincent's at the Staten Island emergency room location when I arrived. Still fretting that they were cutting my brand-new bathing suit—*we ladies know how tough it can be to find the right one*—they prepared my skull for the traction. A steel device that looks like the letter C (aptly named, Crutchfield tongs), it has pins or screws to attach to the skull bone. But, oh the process. The application of this was: "Shave the scalp on the sides of the head." *I can still hear the scraping of the blade as it crossed my temple to remove my hair. In fact, I can still remember that a doctor put his hand over my eyes, so I wouldn't see what they were about to do.* Then, they fit the tongs onto the parietal bones and used a special drill point with a shoulder to enable an exact depth of the hole to be drilled. "Be careful not to impair circulation, avoid excessive manipulation because poor placement can cause flexion/extension forces, and the patient can get occipital decubitus." Oh, dear Lord! Thank you for putting the perfect doctor, Doctor Leventhal, at the hospital, exactly when I needed this skill set. Thank you, because it all started there.

He decided that I should be moved to the St. Vincent's downtown location, as in West Village, New York City. I arrived early morning the next day because the ambulance could travel no more than ten miles per hour. So, they traveled eighteen miles, which even in New York City traffic should take one hour to one hour and thirty minutes, in heavy traffic. My ambulance ride took four hours, and this was at two a.m. It was long and tiresome. I remember a different emergency tech in that second ambulance holding my hand and giving me locations that he could see out the window as we passed by the Verrazano Bridge, and then the tunnel into the city. He also was assuring me that everything is going to be okay. Just hang on.

Sirens and lights were flashing as I made my grand entrance into New York City with forty pounds of metal. This device was drilled into my head and connected to a pulley system—to us this was crazy.

9

There were so many questions, unimaginable to our world, this was. The doctors told me that I must stay this way! Lying flat, and not moving was extremely difficult, especially when all you want to do is scream and wake up from this nightmare! That is, mentally screaming, "Did this just happen, did it?" I did not have a choice. It was funny because this head device is also screaming, and it's demanding, "Don't move." And I think I remember the doctor saying, "Now dear, try not to squirm or——." I screamed. I say "I screamed" a lot because that is all that came out of my mouth for a while. Usually, with a few choice words attached.

"Okay Laurie, this head traction is to prepare you for the surgery and then we will install the Halo?" Lord, have mercy! Install? I remember thinking, I'm f*%kd—this is very real. Yeah, I said it again, I am in so much trouble!

HIP BONE CONNECTED TO MY NECK BONE ♫

Straight-up was my focus, not as in future endeavors but as in the ceiling that I am staring at for hours. It needed painting, and the large spidery cracks became my new friends. They became figures of people or animals at times, as in cloud-watching. I was quickly learning, and I knew every inch of my new home. There were three large windows, to my right, and fifty-eight blinds on each window. I developed great peripheral vision. It is amazing what happens to other senses and mind games you develop when other body parts do not work.

Three days it took my mom to travel back to New York City, not with promised, fancy Euro presents, but back to New York City, to her eighteen-year-old girl. A quadriplegic? "Catherine, come home," my uncle told his sister. "What happened to Laurie?" "It's very serious, just come home now." He said this and hung up on her purposely, so he did not have to try to explain all that happened. Moms had to stop her plans and trip and find someone to help her go back on the train, right away, back to something awfully bad. It was better that she didn't know exactly what had happened. Exactly that her daughter hit her head on the bottom of a pool, and she is paralyzed.

It's overwhelming, all that is thrown at you in the first seconds of meeting the medical doctors who are treating your loved one. The ability to separate yourself from the nightmare that brought you to a hospital and the amount of brain power now needed to understand all that the doctors are saying is huge. I remember her questions, her confusion, her frustration; she was mad, afraid. "Your daughter is a quadriplegic, she will never walk again," Doctor Ho, the on-staff neurosurgeon at St. Vincent's New York City, told her when she arrived—she was exhausted from her travels—I heard her scream.

She held onto Marie, her younger cousin. Mom used to tell me dear stories about being Marie's babysitter. They were close, and when Marie came home from medical school, mom had a dinner to welcome her home. What is going to happen to Laurie, that's all she cared about now.

"They are going to take a piece of her pelvic hip bone and put it in the spot of the injury to fuse it, secure the bone structure." The reality of the surgery was far more complicated than explained, but those were the basics. All of this was more than could be understood. Anyway, the surgery was scheduled.

"Will she walk again? Will she move? Will she? She had so many questions, and my mother thankfully had Marie to help her understand. Sadly, my future was going to be complicated. Doctors go with statistics, and in my case a C-6 incomplete neck fracture held doubtful chances of moving, or walking ever again, so my odds weren't good.

So many open-ended questions. So many unsure results. One thing we knew, that it was going to be a difficult life now. Less than one percent of such people can walk again, hence the gloomy prognosis of Doctor Ho, he was going with the safe bet.

FORK IT

So now I need surgery, they will take bone from my pelvic bone and fuse it into the broken part, the neck part—the C6 incomplete fracture. That's the *Dummies* version. The body is so incredible, so complicated and marvelous. That is, if it works correctly, but as soon as it shuts down, well, then you resort to forks, yes, forks, dinner forks, cake forks, whatever! My mother told me years later that in the first few weeks, she used to stick my legs with hospital forks and knives to see if they would respond. Desperation!

"Laurie, the priest is here to see you." So? I was in a Catholic hospital, but this was not the resident priest. He was the head guy at the born-again church, and he told me that he had had a dream about me! When he walked in, he flinched as soon as he saw me, like everyone else did. Why did it bother me? Maybe because I had forty pounds of weights with a C-clamp *in* my head, attached to my head! I was an early Nautilus machine! Or, as a friend just told me, I looked worse than Frankenstein, so much worse.

As I lay there listening to him, he told me that God had showed him a young girl with red hair in a hospital room. We had never met. He sat and befriended me, and he told me stories of his wife, his sons, grandchildren, their picnics; he was a sweet man, with a kind face. I like this priest. This man from the non-denominational church. It was getting late and he had his son waiting in the car for him.

He said before he left that he had to do what God had showed him to do. When he prayed, I was already looking up. It's true, isn't it? We all think of God as in a direction of "up," in heaven. I could not move at all laterally, or side to side. So, he opened my fist, it was like the hand of a stroke victim, closed and tight, and typical of quadriplegics. And he began praying, the C-traction held my fixed direction.

Eyes wide open and keeping my focus up, I said to God, "Whatever I did to deserve this, I am sorry." Reverend Mercaldo said—"NO, God did not cause this as punishment. He continued to pray, and I felt heat and an electric type of shock move upward from my hand and higher up the whole arm area, then into my collar bone area. Below that, nothing. Funny thing to describe paralyzed. No, it's not like when your elbow hits the funny bone. It is nothing. No feel. No move. Nothing. He smiled and said that he would come back and visit next Saturday night.

He did come back to visit me, for the next three Saturday afternoons. He gave me a New Testament "Good News" blue hardcover bible. I still have it. He wrote a note which said, "Follow your journey with God. Trust Him to lead you and guide you."

Sunday, the very next day, on an endless, hot Indian summer morning, I was lying in bed and I heard, "Move your toe." —This phrase was loud and clear to me, I was alone in the room, I was the only one who heard it. Hundreds of times I heard it. Hundreds. It wasn't audible, but more like a deafening sound of something that won't stop. Well, it didn't stop; a few hours into this, until I paused to try. I tried to know if I could even tell if my left pinky toe was on my left foot or if my left foot was even there attached to my leg—let alone move it. Feeling was a whole new effort. They told me to forget this gift, they told me, "No, you will not. You cannot." Well, that's what they said, and it was all that they knew.

I zeroed in on my toe with my brain. It was there, it had a presence, like an outline of something, I just can't find the details. Minutes went by, seemed like hours, I felt the toe, felt to move it. I screamed.

MOM! She was in the hall. She came running in, she looked, she screamed as she watched me move my toe, and she ran out. She ran back with Debbie Green, the head nurse, also our favorite nurse on staff. Debbie looked, she also screamed, and they both ran out to call the resident doctor on call. Three hours later, he showed up to say, "Oh—we forgot to mention, you will have muscle spasms—involuntarily."

"NO, no—she moved that damn toe, I saw it myself." Debbie "professionally" screamed at him.

SHATTERED

The damage was at the C6 level of the cervical spine. Writing this now, I still get a weird sensation at that level in my neck as I am realizing that I had hit my head so hard that a piece of my bone snapped, splintered, or shattered? How gross, how freaking gross.

Doctor Leventhal had scheduled a pre-op meeting to explain the surgery. I briefly remember meeting him, I even wonder if I was coherent enough to understand him—a lot was going on and I just remember his kind smile, the rest was now on my mom. She had arrived late the night before, just in time from her long journey. Mom did get the help she needed in Zürich. She had to rush back and get her things and tell her travel group, as they were eating steak and frites. This trip to Europe was a kickstart into her new life now as a young widow. My father had a major heart attack and had stomach cancer. He died three years earlier, in 1976. She was supposed to go enjoy herself and find her confidence again, to find her way, she was 43, with three teenagers and she was single. It was happening for her until she was directed to a phone call waiting for her from home.

The first thirty-six hours were endless, with doctors, nurses, catheters, tubes, machines, IV's, the lights, and the fogginess because of so much morphine! Grunting, crying for necessities—!! Peeing, pooping! They said I can't do that anymore. My body! It doesn't work anymore. Oh my God, what am I going to dooooooo—how can I live again, how, why, where, when? —someone tell meeeeeeeeeeeee! They prepared us as much as possible for the surgery that I needed. They did their best to assure us that the procedure to repair the broken bone and to stabilize the neck was just that. There was no surgery that could repair a damaged spinal cord.

They scheduled a date for the following Monday, next week for the fusion surgery. We were all set, but that Friday night I spiked a temperature of 105.1. Being that I was already weak, the fever was not a good thing to happen a few days before surgery. After an all-night battle and around eight pounds of ice dumped in the bed with me, they decided to do a spinal tap! So scary and so unnecessary. One doctor suggested that I might have contracted spinal meningitis and ordered the tap! "What is going on over there?" When my surgeon found out that they did this, he was so upset! It is a dangerous procedure because they have to insert a needle into your spinal cord to remove the fluid, without touching it or cause any other damage! They bent me over as much as they could, and I remember crying. I asked the doctor who was doing the procedure if he would be careful, and he showed me the four vials he just filled, while he was talking to me. He was finished, and we all were relieved. I did not have meningitis, I had a spinal cord injury and happened to get a fever. Results were clear, I was rescheduled for the following week.

IS THIS HEAVEN?

But, a voice, again I hear? It repeatedly voiced for me to **move your toe**, your paralyzed toes? The toes that the doctors said you would never move again, and which you didn't know were even there since this all had happened. And now it moves, your toe has a presence and they said you would never—? I surrender to that, emphatically, that whether you know Him or not, you give the credit and glory to God! End of questions there. Trust me—. Now, the hope, the dream of walking or even moving, even feeling the essence of a body part again, or just knowing it is even there, existing, inside your body, outside your body, this dream now has a chance! A week later, when the fever was totally gone, the surgery was done. They took a slice of my right pelvic bone and put it in the broken cervical bones in my neck. Fusion!

Post-surgery, I woke up in a white room, and I heard soft singing. "Is this heaven?" I wonder. Well, I did wake up with a Halo on! No, this isn't heaven, it was just the surgical nurse who was preparing for my wake-up. I forget his name, but he came right over when I almost pulled the tube that felt deep into my stomach. He yelled at me. "Crazy girl you cannot pull your tube, you need it to breathe for few more days! Oh, and don't try to scream or talk. You will have to talk to us using this alphabet sheet. Point to the letters to make words for the next two days."

Is he kidding! I could move my arm, but my fingers weren't moving. I could hardly even see, after this six-hour (?) surgery. I'm thirsty, I am—*Wait a minute I have to check, can I feel anything now? Did the surgery work? There was no question that we all thought or hoped this would help me walk, they did explain that it wouldn't, but still—. It's natural, I did go into the surgery moving my toe! And moving my arms, which was great. But was I going to walk? It was always the question, always the hope.*

So important, this, is my first reality check! Was it too early to give up hope? Was it too early to accept this, to accept that I will never be the same person, and or I will never walk again?

Are you in a demanding situation? It is try-or-die time. Those two choices, always, just two—so simple yet so demanding. Demanding of a choice to either *get up* or *stay down, go for it* or *get forgotten— attempt* or *fail, it is one direction* or *another*, it's the *at least you tried, get out of your own way* attitude *that counts*. If you are lying around talking to yourself and wasting time, wasting talents, dragging in your dirt of _?_, fill in the blank_____? This choice had you defeated at "Why bother?" It defeated you at "It's too hard." Even though your challenge may not be as difficult as mine are, undoubtedly you will need to make this type of choice for yourself. Don't expect anyone else to take you by the hand and make it all go away.

INSTALLATION SUCCESSFUL

Luckily, I was under anesthesia when they *put* the Halo into my head. It was a steel circle with holes for the five screws that they implanted into my skull. I kept asking, "Is there enough room between my skin and my skull for a screw to go in? Where are you putting them? How can this be?" Yes, they did, they drilled into my skull and put those four screws into the circle and metal bars attached to a vest. It all weighed around thirty pounds. Later, one screw had to be removed because it got infected and a new location was drilled for the fifth location. Installation was successful.

The Halo traction was the most tormenting part of this circus. And it was difficult to even look at me. At least I knew this by the reactions from people who came to visit. These were my family, my friends and even the staff. My friend referred to the C-clamp traction as worse than Frankenstein. This latest look, the Halo, put me at a thousand times worse than that. It was so bad that no one was allowed to bring a mirror in their purse or show me in anyway what I looked like. My mother made sure of this since it became quite upsetting. I kept screaming, "What do I look like!" No one told me the truth, they couldn't find the words.

Fortunately, I did not have to depend on the nursing staff at St. Vincent's because my mother's insurance paid for twenty-four-hour nursing care. (Insurance companies sure changed that.) St. Vincent's was an aging hospital and was not equipped for spinal cord injuries. Three shifts of private RNs were sent to nurse me. I remember seeing them come in the room, all with *that similar look*, and I could *see* them thinking, "Oh my, did I study spinal cord injury in nursing school? This girl is messed up—she cannot sit up, she cannot lift hand to mouth, let alone use her fingers to hold a spoon or fork. She cannot do anything!"

I overheard this rambling by more than one of the nurses sent to "nurse" Me. "Well, hello...this is why you're here?" They were so uncomfortable attending to me, it was obvious. Really, all they had to do was feed me, sponge and bathe me, check my urine bag, catheter me—uh, check for bowel movements, which goes beyond question, doesn't it? But—back in 1979, spinal cord injuries were rare, even professionals weren't prepared for everything. By the end of their shift with me, I would tell them whether or not to come back. I fired about five of those nurses before the best ones decided to commit to this with me.

I wasn't exactly a great patient. I screamed a lot and I did not sleep for sixty-one plus days. I was so glad for my brave, new nurse, Bernice. A small woman, "from the Islands," she used to say. I asked her every day, which island? Jamaica? Antigua? She used to smile and say *not important, you are*—. She had a great long-suffering strength to deal with me. I am grateful for her. Bernice stayed with me until I left St. Vincent's, it was, more like she endured me and all my junk, until I was released!

In the mornings, it was important to me that my legs were moved. My legs *hurt* so badly and the "return" of nerve signals and muscle tone coming back alive was so—unnerving. Ha! I cried to have them moved by anyone. I wasn't picky about who did it, just as long as my legs were stretched and taken out of the *fixed* spasm. There are a few types of spasms that I experienced early on. The shaking kind, where your body part shakes so uncontrollably—you'd better watch out, they have a force of amazing power that can-do leg kick movements, Bruce Lee style. This type can jerk you out or off the bed. It did happen. Luckily, I had enough arm strength to grab the bar and get back on the bed. And then there are the stiff or fixed type of spasms, which are almost worse—not sure if a comparison can be fair, but the stiff type is the equivalent of a supernatural glue, you cannot move. Even with other hands, trying to help unlock your legs or arms or torso, it is an insane strength of those muscles that are keeping you held in bondage—scream!

My first class of the day at St. Vincent's Hospital was "Breathing 101." I remember the respiratory therapist whose name was, of all names, Jesús. He was the first college graduate in his family, and with a huge smile, he told me stories every morning, delightful stories of his grandfather and his uncles. He was so proud of his Puerto Rican heritage. I think he thought that if he kept telling me how much he had overcome, how hard he and his family had worked to achieve wonderful things, that I would be encouraged.

Jesús showed me the device with the balls in it. It looked like one of those old-fashioned coin counters. It had four vertical tubes, with a ball in each tube. Or, it looked like the machine with the numbered lottery balls, where the balls dance around at the bottom and then air pushes them to go straight up. That was my task of the day. I had to be the air machine. It took me weeks to get one ball up the tube. That's how I got to know Jesús. Every morning, he whistled a tune as he came to torture me. Sometimes he was cheery to the point of nausea. I struggled with my breathing. And boy, did he have fun with that verbiage. "Blow. Laurie, you've got to breathe when you blow." If there is a Jesús out there who worked in St. Vincent's, who was a respiratory therapist in 1979, I wish you well, dear brother. Thank you for your encouragement and a job well done.

"To Pee or Not to Pee?" That was really the bigger question or task of the morning, and that was my next class. I was blessed incredibly early on in this nightmare, about the fourth week, with the ability and knowledge to pee. This means I knew my bladder was full. I knew, and I could sense or feel, and I got that little urge you get when you must pee. This very thing is huge, people! Basic body functions were all the day's efforts for me at this time and a measure or barometer of how things were going to be that day. Either the body cooperated and worked, or I was going to need a catheter that morning. Or was it a day of hope because your bladder was working so well that you can tell WHEN THE BAG GETS RIPPED OUT OF YOU—yes, this happened twice! All this bladder and urinary knowledge was a huge accomplishment. I was in training mode. I was training my mind and bladder to coincide the urge and the ultimate. The tiny but major meatus muscle—that when it works, the pee comes out when you want it to and you feel the warmth of your own urine, which was a good thing at the time. Each drop into the bedpan was sheer delight. Imagine. With a basic function like peeing, what was my final exam going to be like? This was all we thought about. I say, "we" because it was everyone's question of the day, it seemed.

I was slowly showing signs of improvement, although the honeymoon was far from over. Hospital life and the newness of my situation were killing me. The harshness of not being able to move, this was a new life. The doctors, the nurses, the medications, the routine of tubes and needle pricks. I remember them taking blood for twenty-eight days straight. Finally, after seeing my arm with black, green and blue tie-dye stains, I asked, "Why? Do you know why you are taking blood?" The tech did not, I told him to find out. He never came back! I was tired of this already, it was hot. It was already fall and still in the 80's. There was no air conditioning, just ceiling fans. This was all worthy of a long damn scream. Shock!

DID I REALLY SPEAK THIS WAY?

At that time, most of my friends were eighteen and entering their freshman year of college, usually an age of self-discovery for most. I hated it! I hated that they were out there. I was jealous. I was trapped in two prisons, inside this hospital and inside my body. My time of self-discovery for the last two months was "this," this new semester of quad life, it was all focused-on movement. Or lack of it. I was a freshman in Spinal Cord Injury, and I was wanting to drop this class the first chance I could get.

My friends' perspective about my accident has brought some clarity but also raised many questions. Did I really seem positive? Did I speak and make others feel like I was going to be fine? When was this? Who was this person described here? Some old friends, from grammar school and high school buddies, wrote to me recently. What I absolutely love is that their memories do confirm some of mine—now I know the craziness was real!

Joanne T., 4/10/2017

Hi Laurie,

It was good to catch up the other day. I also called Margherita to see what she remembered about our visit to you at the Rusk Institute.

As we talked about, I remember that it was a beautiful sunny day when we came to see you in the hospital. I was nervous and didn't know what to expect. I wasn't sure if you would know who we were, if you were paralyzed, or even wanted to see anyone. We hadn't really kept in touch much since St. Simon & Jude. When we walked in, I remember the "Halo" contraption that you were attached to that had screws imbedded in your head. I had never seen that or knew anyone who had broken his/her neck. It was scary looking, and it wasn't clear whether it caused you any pain. When you began talking to us I remember feeling relieved because you described what happened to you and that you knew you weren't going to die because of the white light that appeared to be reaching for you. You were very hopeful about your recovery. I'm sorry I don't remember your words, but, I do remember that you had a feeling or faith that everything would be okay. That was a relief to me and Margherita too. When I asked if she remembered any details, she said she remembered being uncomfortable at first as we were approaching your room, but, after we visited she felt you were going to be okay.

I wish I could remember more than that. All I can say is that you were hopeful and optimistic and that put us at ease.

We had a reunion of sorts a couple of years later – somewhere near Nellie Bly I think. Marion C was there (she went to Dewey with you?) and you walked in using 2 canes and I was so happy that you were able to walk again!

That is about all I remember. I am glad you are writing about it – I know it's hard and emotional, but, you are and will be an inspiration to others.

Stay well, my friend, and let's do better about keeping in touch.

Marion C.

Laurie-

Can't remember how I found out. I assume someone called me. – Your mom being so depressed and somber.

So, unlike her. She had an extremely tough time in the beginning. But as you improved, so did she.

Bess, moisturizing your hands. She was going to nursing school. I thought to myself, Bess? She didn't know you well enough to be rubbing you down. I was a bit jealous! This was at St. Vincent's.

I also remember you blowing the ball up in the container for your breathing. It was the first time I saw that. That was at St. Vincent's too. - I think we visited you in groups, as we did everything. So, it was me and Barbara and Maureen. Once a month or so. - I also remember that new friend of yours at Rusk/NYU, Claudia. I think you stayed in touch with her. You still may be in touch. I do remember driving to NYU and the parking lot which is no longer there. Happy to talk more about it. That may help. Remember this... it's a story of triumph!"

Love, Marian

Jackie B.

A series of starts and stops as I tried to complete it at various times, so please disregard the choppiness. Perhaps more than you asked for or less. I just wanted to put out there the things that stood out in my memory going back to that time. Love you, sister, and wishing you good things and much success with your book."

This is what I remember....

We all went to New Paltz. I think it was supposed to be a girl's weekend, if I remember correctly. You couldn't make it and stayed local. I think that your mom was traveling. I know we went, but don't ask me who. Of course, Maureen and Marion were there, and I think that girl Wendy and a few others. We missed you. We didn't find out that anything happened until after we got home. I think it was sometime later that week.

I got a phone call from Bess Mancino and she told me the news. She said, "Laurie broke her neck". I remember being stunned. I had never heard of that happening before. Of course, I have heard people say stuff like "if continue to do this or that, I'll break your neck," or "You better watch out or you'll break your neck."

I knew it was serious, but I didn't realize how serious and that the effects would be long lasting. Sometimes I am an idiot. I also think that it was much too painful to think otherwise. My beautiful friend Laurie, who was always so easy to be around, with an easy laugh. Who always made me laugh and who enchanted people wherever we went.

I am sorry, Laur, but I remember thinking that maybe, it would not have happened if you came with us that weekend. Everything about it scared me. It just reinforced in me the feeling that everything is so fragile and that all things are out of our control. I am predisposed to thinking this way anyway, I guess, because of my own life experiences.

Ok, I am crying now.

I visited you in the hospital. You were in bed and you had that chrome metal brace around your head that appeared to be screwed to your head. You were thirsty, and someone held a cup of water to your lips for you to drink from a straw. Then you went to the rehabilitation center. I don't remember seeing you while you were there, but you must have worked awfully hard. Shortly after you came home, you had the girls at your house. You were walking with two canes. Amazing!!

The entire crew was there and then the doorbell ring. You asked me to get it, so I did. There was a limousine outside and the girl that you met at the rehabilitation center was there. Her chauffeur had helped her to the door. I think she was in a wheelchair. I remember that we all had a wonderful day. It seemed to us that nothing had changed, but that was only because of the person you are.

At some point, you and I discovered that we both had an affinity for the music of Neil Young. I was introduced to his music by my rock and roll LI friends and you, by folks at the rehab center (at least, I think so). I think you used to smoke doobs [doobies] hanging out listening to Neil.

I may be getting the chronology wrong, but this is what else I remember, just maybe not in order. I didn't know how much time had passed, but I don't think very much. We gathered the girls together for a trip up to New Paltz. You did and went everywhere we did.

The day we decided to walk the trail to the falls at Lake Minnewaska was a stretch, though. But you came with us anyway, although your means of travel was a bit different. The night before at a bar, you had met a nice and cute guy—(what else is new)—that was smitten with you. He drove you near the top of the falls and carried you on his back all the way up to our meeting point. Really so amazing.

Either before that or after I remember visiting you at your dorm at FIT in New York City.

I tell you, Laurie, you were so brave and bold, you never let the accident and this disability stop you. You never complained, ever, that I recall.

Of course, then you met Paul, the love of your life, got married and had a son.

Love you and hope to see you soon,

Jackie

Maureen F.

Hey Laurie,

Sorry it's taken me so long to get this to you. This must be so hard for you; it's been painful for me (for you) to recall this so I can't even imagine.

I remember vividly the first time I went to see you in the hospital after I found out about your accident. Perhaps because I was young and not familiar with the severity of neck and back injuries, I wasn't prepared for the way you looked when I saw you in the hospital. Naively (and stupidly!) I bought magazines for you thinking that would be something you could do. I imagined it but the look on your face when I handed them to you was incredulous (in a subtle way) like, are you f*&##ing kidding me...how can I read right now!).

I remember standing on the left side of your bed, your bed was near the window and your Mom was on the other side of the bed sobbing, "My beautiful baby; my beautiful girl". I felt so so bad for her (and you) but now that I'm a Mom I can understand the horrible anguish and heart-breaking pain she must have been in. I remember that she had been traveling in Europe and was gone just a brief time when you got hurt.

I remember how frail you looked, which took me aback because we were all were tough, mighty, invincible dancing queens who danced upstairs in Jackie's bedroom and your living room to Che Che La Fa, hitching rides all over Brooklyn (even Manhattan).

I'm glad we're still friends after all these years. We need to plan another pool party. (I promise, no mixing drinks!) I love you.

Christine L.

It was 1979, the year we graduated from high school. A mutual high school friend, who relocated to Arizona that summer called to check in sometime in the fall. She delivered the news that Laurie had been in an accident -- a pool accident. My first reaction was that she had drowned. I don't recall much of the details, but, that she was in the hospital, suffering from severe damages. I called around and found out she was at St. Vincent's Hospital in Greenwich Village.

It sounded like she wasn't in a good place, I asked my boyfriend at the time to take me into the city to visit her. Not being aware of the severity of her condition from the accident, I thought I should bring her something to pick up her spirits. We stopped at a new place call the 'Erotic Bakery' on Christopher Street. You can guess the types of pastries and chocolate they sell -- all in X-rated shapes. I remember choosing the largest chocolate shaped p**** filled with cream. I thought that she would definitely get a kick out of this treat!

I remember entering her hospital room and saw her mom, who endearingly, we call Mumsie. She looked tired and broken. She sat vigil. When I turned and saw Laurie, I completely froze. In my head, I hadn't pictured much but that I would see her lying in her hospital bed. It was more compelling than that -- when I saw all the tubes, and metal hardware holding her body, particularly supporting her neck and head in place. I was stunned because I didn't realize that she was paralyzed. She was unable to turn her head, let alone move any parts of her body. When we made eye contact, we both couldn't hold back the tears. I was afraid to touch her, because I didn't want to hurt her. I imagined it may have felt like death for her inability to feel. Before leaving, I told her I bought her something cheerful. I tilted the box of 'chocolate.' I saw briefly, a teary smile.

I continued to visit Laurie and ended up in college together. As the years went by, we became closer and developed a more meaningful friendship, far from our casual years in high school . I've witnessed her strength and courage as she slowly progressed in her mobility to walking and gaining quality of life with her disability. I was always completely in awe of how she managed to carry a baby to full term and delivered naturally. I also have deep admiration for Mumsie and her husband Paul -- one who never left her side, and one who will forever be by her side. They are the backbone of her success. She's an exemplary example of courage, along with faith that one can achieve and become *fit - able.*"

My friends' memories are meaningful in every way. They were there to support me when I left in-patient status and helped me re-adjust to the world again, they tried to help me see that I was still the same girl, which look Laurie—you can use different methods to get around, (a large statement in such few words), guess I did, looks like I made it up to that peak, even if it was on the back of some new beau! But really, this was all new, I was going to have to say yes to people who offer help. Something that was difficult, especially at eighteen.

MOVING ON UP

"You're going to Rusk!" Doctor Howard Rusk was a pioneer in rehabilitation medicine, and in 1950 he founded the Institute of Rehabilitation Medicine at NYU. Pat told us that I was lucky. She was my patient advocate, and she arranged and searched for a facility where I could get rehab. Not any rehab, I needed the best available. A bed was ready, and it was time to go, time to really see what my future was going to become.

The fourth-floor neuro at St Vincent's was going to be glad I left! The heat that summer in New York City was awful—the perfect reflection of my intense insanity! It was near the end of September, it was supposed to be cooling off, but it was so unusually and insanely hot—*just like me, this wasn't supposed to happen*!

Three screamers on the floor: an older man, who had a stroke, and screaming was the only communication available to him, and a Parisian woman. She had traveled to New York City to surprise her son, and a taxi hit her. She woke up in amnesia speaking only French, not knowing who she was, as her purse was lost at the accident scene. It was hard enough to hear people scream in English, this woman spewed out in French, doesn't matter, the agony is all the same in the cries. "J'ai besoin d'aide," she cried over and over. It sounds like, "I must be dead" in English but it means "I need help!" Or, "Je ne comprends pas" or "I don't understand." It was all sad.

Down the hall, away from all the other patients, there was me. They put me in the only single-bedroom available, it resembled a closet. I was the third screamer. I don't know why I screamed so much—maybe because I couldn't imagine life now, what was I going to do, all the *whys*, and *when's*, and *if only* kept my mind on, twenty-four hours—I had insomnia. No sleep for sixty-one plus days. Insomnia is so strange. The mind is so awake, but my body said, "Please stop." I couldn't, I went over "the day" so many times. I went over the faces, the conversations, those blank stares when I asked, "What will happen to me." I remember lying in bed wondering what

31

my future was going to be. Thinking over and over, "How does one live like this?" I hated this. I hated this. Nothing helped. Drugs, they gave me so many, I remember eleven at each pill swallow. Four times each day, the little, white origami-like cups filled with meds. They didn't work for me. The steroids grew hair on my face. The others? Who knows what they were or supposed to do? All I know is that for someone who couldn't swallow an aspirin before this, I was becoming a pro in pill taking, wow, my big accomplishment! On occasion, I did drift off into a somewhat sleep, usually around four-thirty in the morning. I used to listen to the clock radio in my room, it flipped the minutes, I listened to it for hours, every flip was time passing, a new second in time. Every flip meant this was really happening. Then every morning around five o'clock, the curtain would be pulled back and I would hear, "Psst, Laurie," they whispered, "time to take your TAGAMET." That pill is used to help calm my stomach for all the other pills I was going to have to take that day. Scream!

"We all have a test, but they never come in a form we would like

or prepare for"

—quote from the movie, "The Edge"

The early morning November air hit my face as they put me in an ambulance to go across town to NYU. I thought, "Wow, I haven't been outside since the summer, and now it is freezing!" They tried to cover me as much as possible, but the Halo made it impossible for any head covering, so they hurried me inside the van.

"Welcome, Laurie, to The Institute of Rehabilitation Medicine," my new vocational counselor, Tamar Martin said. "It's the best place for you since you are now having "return." That's when your nerves and muscles are trying to come back alive. I was glad, I was leaving incompetency to go to a medical Shangri la. I was going to run out of Rusk Institute of Rehab Medicine, just wait and see!

"What are you doing," I asked the nurse who was doing my initial evaluation and admittance. She was opening the snaps to the jacket attached to the Halo! "No one ever did this at St. Vincent's," I said. She shockingly looked at me—. "You mean never? No one has ever opened this jacket since they put it on you?" No, I said. I could see the panic in her eyes, she was frightened as to what she was going to find. No bed sores!! I said I never had them, fondly remembering Bernice, who put lotion on me every night. She said, "You're lucky. You're going to find a lot of things done around here that are different."

HOPE WITH A NEW TWIST!

"Good morning! Hey, can you do a leg extension?" a new whitey just asked me. "What does that mean," I asked her. "You know, kick your leg straight out," she replied. "Hi, my name is Donna Twist, ha-ha, funny name for a PT, right? I will be your therapist here starting tomorrow!" She was cute and smiled as she spoke to me. I loved her I-Dream-of-Jeannie-esque ponytail. I did the extension, sort of. I could raise my leg around 10-20 degrees, not full extension, but I moved it! I was trying to get used to moving again. I was trying to remember how to move. Right now, it feels like it's twilight zone for this body, it's lights out!

It was exciting and exhausting at the same time. All the parts were not moving upon request. Some movements set off spasms, some movements never showed up! A lot of mental work, self-talk, they call it now. I just thought I was a little cray cray because I used to and still do, speak to my body parts, sometimes I bark at this body!

My new PT wrote something on the clipboard in her hands. Then she leaned over, and got as close to my ear as possible, and whispered, *"You're going to walk,"* and she ran out of the room. Hey!!!!! I screamed, who was that? She just said I was going to walk! It took me a few seconds to comprehend this.

I mean, she did not say, that was a good leg extension and it is a good thing, that you feel and could move a little. No, it was the completeness of it all, she said "walk"! That is huge, that is everything.

The nurses ran in the hallway, but they could not find this cute blonde, the physical therapist with the ponytail as I described—the only person to say the most important and hopeful words that I heard in two months. Finally! Someone who was excited to see my moves. Yes, I like this place—I was right, I was going to run out of here. But who was that therapist?

This very first evening was interesting when cookies and juice were being given out at the intermission of "Jeopardy." A male nurse was whistling the famous theme music as he rolled a cart of juice, milk and Oreos. Since I'm not a huge fan of Oreos, to his surprise I had some juice and went to sleep.

That is until the last lights were back on now, and a new nurse whistled to the tune of, "Laurie, I'm here to teach you how to catheter yourself!" Wait—oh no. You don't understand—read my chart! I can pee! On my own! "Really." This was not a question, it was the nurse's reaction that first evening, she brought me the smallest size catheter, a chuck, a urinal dish and some betadine solution.

"Since you function so well, young lady, I'll leave this with you and we'll see how you do." Wow, she was tough, and I had no choice but to prove myself before her eyes. So, the bargain was, if I could Cath myself, just this once, she would leave me alone, because then she knew I could do it in case I really *had* to. She left the room. Ha, my chance to show her. I still had the Halo on, so I could not get up to pee, and I also did not even know if I could walk yet. So, I peed in the urinal thing. I avoided the catheter, but I did open the Cath package and betadine and pretended that I did use them! Wrongo—she caught me and so I had to do the deed. I had never tried this at St. Vincent's; they did not even consider it. (They just liked to ignore me and rip the damn thing out of me during transfers.) Well with her watching, maneuvering the Halo in bed, and forty minutes later, I did the Cath, some pee came out, she was happy, and so was I. I never did need to Cath again, and I did have my share of pee accidents, but in SCI reality, I am blessed abundantly.

At 7:45 the next morning, a team of doctors surround my bed. I refer to them as the *whiteys* because of the white coats they all wore. With their charts in hand, they all came to see me this morning. I was a different quad, I moved. First to speak was, "Hi, I am Donna Twist, your physical therapist," she smiled. "It's her! The girl from yesterday who said I would walk," I thought to myself. I still wasn't believing the walking part. But she was sure! A new friend. She is hopeful, the only *whitey* so far. This is a good thing. Now I have something to wake up for and be doing. Something to hold on to and hope for in those endless dark nights.

WORK IT, GIRL!

So now it's the late fall semester, and I *really should be back at school*! I did attend NYU, but not the college program, I was in Physical Therapy, second floor, at NYU-Rusk Institute, nine a.m. to three p.m. every day, to learn how to walk again. How to hold a spoon or fork, how to tie my shoes, how to get into the shower, and how to figure out all of this—how to be independent for the rest of my life.

Here, my new life course at Rusk was "Transfer 101." I had to get used to how things were done here. When they called for PT, I was anxious about this. I had the Halo on and I was top-heavy. Leave me alone on the bed for a few seconds and I am tipping. It happened, at my previous location. To my horror, I face-planted into the bed with my thirty-pound friend attached to my head! Lord have mercy!

I had to learn how to get into my new form of transportation. A wheelchair was put next to the bed, and for this transfer, a small but solid nurse weighing in at around 115 pounds, at the most, came to help with this task. I was waiting for the others, and she laughed when I told her that at St. Vincent's, it took six men and they lifted me in a bedsheet! How polar of an experience. Rusk was rehab-serious. Everything was focused on you, your abilities and how you are going to survive this monumental task of coping in the stress of your new situation. Everyone here was learning. In this course, "Transfer 101," you started from your hospital bed in a lying-down or supine position and rose, or usually be pulled up from your arms to a sitting position, (still a major effort). This small nurse used something resembling a skateboard without the wheels! This transfer board is shoved under the tuchus, (for my New York friends), and you shimmy across the board somehow, anyway you can, into the wheelchair next to the bed. I think that took weeks to accomplish. Everything took weeks or months to do.

The next course was "Mat Class 101," where I had to learn how to get on all fours. Another position so useful for "important future events." The purpose was to strengthen my leg muscles, and hopefully my torso, the old term for core. Balance was also a crucial factor in the sense that I needed to get stronger so that I could balance my body weight to walk. There's a science behind this all. Rehabilitation was my life for this season. I learned so much about myself and my new body. Rehabilitation is still my life. For many seasons now...I am still learning about myself and my new body.

"You're a C-6 incomplete quad." They called me this. I used to wonder, why was this called an incomplete fracture? Incomplete meant the spinal cord was not severed, but damaged. Just a bruise in the cord would swell it and cause the disconnection. But I had more than a bruise. Certainly, there was enough damage done. I thought, "I am still kind of paralyzed." That was complete enough for me.

I get stuck here. I could go into deep and technical medical explanations of physical medicine, or I could try to put you right in that place of shock, and trauma. I was in a unique situation. I did have great return, I did regain a huge amount of my body movement, just not one hundred percent, and this missed mark just killed me. It still does.

LONG DAYS AND LONGER NIGHTS

Days in therapy were getting long. Days were weeks, weeks were then months. In the morning, before dressing, there were those sounds of a hospital. You know, breakfast carts being pushed, nurses hurrying around, getting their patients ready for their day. It's a lengthy process to get a quad or even para up from sleep, catheter, showered in a shower chair, back to transfer in bed to get dressed. The aides took over, they dried you, powdered you, put lotion on you, put your bra on, undies, shirt, pants, socks, tied shoes. Brushed your teeth, brushed your hair—got you ready for the day!

"We are learning life again," I used to think. Like a child. Breakfast, what a chore. Lift, if you can, the lid to cold eggs, wet bacon and some other things that seemed edible, but cereal was safe! That also meant your Rice Krispies weren't going to snap, crackle and pop because they are drenched in milk because the nurses' aide had three others in your room to get ready also, in a hurry, she usually dumped way too much milk.

See, things like this used to drive me crazy. Because I now had to depend on people to do the smallest things. At age eighteen, the norm is to be independent of parents now! Get a job or go to college, and you are getting ready to fly the coop soon! Oh man, there is more than just chicken wires holding me back, I have a steel Halo. I'm totally grounded for now. I just got pushed back a while on any dreams.

I loved being the first one ready, and I was always eager to go to therapy. I felt like these *whiteys*, the therapists, were the only ones who totally understood the dilemmas. They understood, our limitations, our "NO, it doesn't work anymore" cries! Well, those were mine. I was trying so hard to just "sit up." I was relearning how to get my fingers to open and close buttons, do zippers, and all those small intricate moves. Occupational therapy was a blessing and a curse at times. My fingers and hands were very weak and needed extra help via the mostly unpleasant of inventions, hand splints. VELCRO© did find its diamond mine in a hospital. I was taped up and un taped so many times.

At night when I should have been sleeping, usually I was up, annoyed at these devices intended to straighten my fingers because they were also destroying my cheeks with every touch to my face. You can imagine what it was like when I had to use the bathroom. So, I usually hung the splints next to me on the bed, and right before morning rounds I would put them back on, except one time. I did not wake up and rounds came early. My OT was not empathetic and tormented me until I had no options but to do what I had to do and wear the darn things all night!

My right hand is almost normal-looking and functions at about ninety-five percent well. The left hand? Working at about sixty percent and not so straight. The fingers stay folded, but they do work, and it's just the least of my troubles. I think I had put all my efforts into walking again, it was so much harder and demanding and so natural to want to move again to walk.

HALO SIGHTING

I had roommates, and the very first person, besides myself, wearing this Halo was Liz. She was waiting for the elevator, smoking a cigarette, and looking pissed. She was another person who had this thirty-pound headwear! This amazed me, someone else and she was sitting up in a wheelchair and moving around so well. She was cute, and boyish looking, because she had head trauma and they needed to shave her hair—a drunk driver had struck Liz and her boyfriend, and she suffered all these injuries, SCI C6 incomplete, like me, brain injury and some hand loss. That year in 1979, there were nineteen young people all under the age of twenty-one. It was sad to see life sucked out.

I used to say that a lot— "This sucks." I remember the first time I said it to Claudia, another roommate. She had also jumped into a pool, but her body didn't respond like mine. She did have movement, but this is spinal cord injury 101, and they are all different.

Claudia was cool, pretty, smart and someone I could hang with, and we did C, and did have some great escapades for girls like us. Sorry Liz, maybe because you endlessly played the soundtrack from SWEENEY TODD—all day and all night!!! We didn't relate, but I remember your heart, and how you encouraged me to come with you after dinner hours to visit a "young girl" on the pediatrics floor. We did so for a while, but she sadly passed. She was so little, only able to be in a crib! She looked six years old, but she was twenty-four! I remember having a tough time with those visits. But you figured out how to make her feel special, and you did an excellent job. She called us her friends.

But I related more to C—we loved music, but she was like a guru, a real fan, and she knew all the lyrics and the names of songs and the artists who wrote them. Me, I loved music, disco. I know, it was an era, but that's what we did in Brooklyn, we danced on the weekends, it was 1979.

It is now November, and it was Thanksgiving. This usually meant large amounts of food, turkey, stuffing, gravy, sweet potato pie and cranberry crunch! That is the American version, in Italian homes; there is always a lasagna tray somewhere, meatballs and sauce, in case you weren't already noticing your pants were getting tight. My beautiful Mom brought it all to Rusk, she loved to cook, it reminded me of great times, we did have the best dinner parties at my home. Mom started her entertaining for a particular day or holiday at least a week or two in advance. My mom could have had her own TV cooking show for sure. I always say she should have opened a restaurant. Groceries, her tools in the kitchen, the table setting... "from soup to nuts," my uncle used to say. This Thanksgiving, however; we ate with my brother Vinny, in a large cold gray hospital meeting room. There wasn't the yumminess of pumpkin pie in the oven, or a front yard full of red and golden leaves, it was different this year. It was anything but warm and inviting especially for a holiday meal. Mom brought everything for the three of us. She could have fed the entire hospital staff that day, but this was her normal. Like every Italian mom I knew, they would always ask as they came out from the kitchen with platters of food, "Oh did I make enough?" Enough??

My Dad had just died in 1976, I hate the 1970s; our Grandmother died, my father died, my grandfather came to live with us and then he died...my family was shattered and fell into a silence. That was easier. We didn't speak about dad anymore out loud; nor did we speak about his death with a therapist. That type of healing wasn't popular back then. Going to a therapist, meant you really had issues. I missed him so much, I was almost 15; I was not ready for this, for a life without my father...a life now without him in our house that he loved so much. My father's name was Mario. He was Sicilian, all the way, (in Brooklyn terms... both his parents were Italian) and he looked so handsome all the time. When he wasn't working, he was home renovating our house, it was normal to see him breaking down walls, his hair always covered in drywall dust. His talents would have been curated by those home repair shows.

He was one of the original fixer uppers.

Our house was so awesome in the 70s. Life was so good as far as I knew. We had a pretty house, had all the fun stuff we wanted like bikes, skates, bowling balls, pogo sticks, a lot of sports related stuff.

We were the active bunch I guess, but times were simple then. We did school, homework and then went to play outside till dark. When the weather turned cold, we did puzzles and paint by number. I was a little weird; I used to read the World Book Encyclopedias my brothers had displayed, A-Z, on their bookshelves in their room.

It is three months now, technically four since December fourth was a week away and that was my A-day (accident day). Every day was counted, and I kept marking my mental calendar as if I had a date that would end this nightmare. As if I knew the day that I would be strong enough to go home and begin life again! But I had to learn how to change this from a bad memory to the type that says *Do not remember the past but look forward to tomorrow.* Oh, what a motivational message! But honestly, I get it. We need to move on with things and learn how to adapt or adjust. It's the *seeing* part that makes the difference.

Today was a difficult day to be thankful, but we were! We were thankful I was alive, thankful I had movement and hopeful to walk again and regain enough strength to be independent again!

That next week, I got the best news! "The Halo is coming off soon!" What a huge day this will be. I was thrilled and panicked at the same time. I felt like a bicycle being worked on, only no blood pressure test here, this particular nurse came with a set of real tools, screw gun, ratchets and all. He put the screwdriver in reverse and pulled five screws from my skull—I remember what the doctors said before they put it on in surgery: "It is necessary," they said— "to stabilize your neck." Ten weeks of stabilization and I was going to be good. I was going to be okay. Just wait and see what happens when this comes off, this is what I kept telling myself.

There were good days and there were bad days. "I remember that you were pissed but determined!" my physical therapist, Donna Twist, recently reminded me. I guess no one really knew what was going to happen with me. Every spinal cord injury is different, and the differences are huge. Some may get return of their legs, with so many different strengths and weaknesses that it is too difficult to gauge. In one leg, you may get great quadriplegic muscles, but hamstrings or glutes do not return. That would make standing difficult. Some may be able to bring their hand to their mouth, but that's it, and others have no feeling again in most major muscle groups at all. Some may walk again like me, and there are variations within that category. I was even in rehab with Halos who walked! Those people, usually injured in car accidents, were the walking dead to me. They used to hang on the walls when they went out for their walking routines at night. For the first few months I didn't even know they were in the room next to me.

It was funny, they only came out at night almost like a zombie crowd, they had the most faraway look. Heavily medicated for the pain, they needed that type of traction to secure their bones after surgery. It would be temporary, until they were healed enough to remove the Halo. But it was always annoying to see those people walk around with the very same torture that toppled me over and only had one purpose—to secure my neck, but it might not have any added benefits, like the zombie crowd. I mean, it would not help me walk again. I had great challenges ahead of me, and that frustration and "pissed" mode actually motivated me to determine to get past this. That *maybe just maybe* type of hope; that I could keep regaining nerve impulses and muscle strength. I guess that was my game face, and I didn't know I even had one.

Even though I was making huge gains, I went in and out of hope and discouragement. I think I begged Donna to let me go home every single day. Every single day. I used to say, "I gotta get out of here!" To me this was insane, it was so long already—it's four months and counting since my life changed. I remember almost chanting, "*I missed my life, my simple life. I would have done anything to reverse time, to go back to that day, and get a pass. I needed my bedroom, my house, my dog. It all seemed gone, it was gone, my life. The life I knew. I was very athletic, always was. With two older brothers, I was athletic by default because I was the youngest and a girl. I became the catcher in baseball, the defender in basketball and always counted those darn 'Mississippi's' in football!*" I played girls volleyball and softball in elementary school and ran during high school. In fact, I began running four months prior to this mess and was the proud owner of the first edition of women's Brooks running shoes. This was my life, I was excited for my future. I had goals, and expectations. College was less than two weeks away.

QUADTERNITY

I never hear the splash of the water or the exact hit, but I usually remember the realization of what just occurred. I usually remember the pounding inside my head and the heaviness of my head. It just wants to fall backwards and rest. There is no way I could possibly bring it back to neutral. I am trying but it is gone, the ability to control any muscle. The thought process went out, but the signal from my brain stops, it seems gone into **QUADTERNITY**. That place of .... A schooling of quadriplegia in about two seconds. This school's admittance requirements do not take much ability to be admitted because we are all a second or two away from any accidental disaster. But a real two seconds of this new state and you do realize, a harsh reality. I cannot move, literally to save my life.

This happens sometimes. I keep coming back to this. To that exact moment of my A-day when it happened. They call these moments flashbacks. Distinct memories of a moment of trauma. A memory that is a dangerous place to go sometimes but *it* stays, *it* delays leaving, *it* likes to hang on. It's that uninvited guest who shows up on their terms, very unwelcomed.

Like I said before, at the exact moment I must have said, "Jesus"!! As in help! so loudly, that He knew I needed saving. I knew Him as my "faith" but I met Him in a totally other way. He literally heard my cry and saved me from the depth of trouble I was in. He brought me up from the pool bottom and it was Him who brought me back. I say this because some people think it was luck that brought me back, as if I did anything to save myself. I couldn't. I was paralyzed.

Undoubtedly, my life changed in a nanosecond. Now, after all these years, I am convinced that I died and went to a place for a suspended moment. That place and time that God decides where you will be most used. The time of collision with the pool bottom, the time of trauma to the spine and spinal cord, the exact time that all this happened, technically, my body shut down. Paralysis. Spinal cord severed? Quadriplegia. In fact, it was like in "The Matrix," when the crew members got their life lines pulled out. Suddenly, there is no signal, and your reality changes. Your caught up in a new world, it is new and confusing. The program has changed.

MY RESIDENCY

In rehab, I continued doing well, and I was now standing! The Halo was off, and every morning in therapy, I was strapped and tied to a "standing board." The view was so much better! But also frightening because it felt like a headache and stomach cringe from a bad amusement park ride. That took a while to get used to.

We also did a lot of mat work. It reminds me of Pilates mat work, and one of the first goals for me was to sit up on my own. A bigger goal was to be able to stand up and sit down, and that takes a lot of muscles. I was getting schooled in my own anatomy. We were talking "quads, hams, and glutes" way back when. That achievement was huge, and it meant that I could get in and out of bed, a car, a toilet bowl! Oddly, I could also open the milk container. When nurse Marianne saw this, the fact that I spread the little weird part on the top of the carton, and then opened it, she said, "That's it kid, you're on your own. Put on your own socks, bra, tops, and tie your shoes." Really. I was on my way! I was just so glad I could also put on mascara. Marianne was tough, but in an effective way, for me.

Things changed in rehab after four-thirty in the afternoon. All the physical, occupational, and speech therapists went home, and the place went into hospital mode. It was the usual dinner service, five o'clock pill rounds, etc., all to get ready for the evening shift, and boy, did things shift. A new line of nurses and a new line of aides reported for evening duty.

This was *their* shift, and they did things *their* way. Theirs was the *get with the program or be ignored* mode or *I didn't hear your call bell* mode! It always seemed that when you really needed help they were out to lunch or on a break. Usually it was selective call bells that they would answer. I had a challenging time with some of them but managed to get around the bullshit. As a long-term patient, you learn how to fight your battles. I no longer felt like a patient, I felt like a resident.

Later, when I was able to move around and walk, I usually fed myself and other patients or got things for them. I used my wheelchair before I had a cane, I think. I fondly remember another inductee to this new group, a girl from Long Island, a high-quad who could only blink her eyes. She loved Chinese take-out, so we ordered house special or pork fried rice, every Friday night. Her hands were held by splints and VELCRO© taped to the arm rests on her chair, and her torso and legs were strapped to the wheelchair. She had to depend on everyone for everything, even the itch on her nose. I figured that I had hands that worked, and I had legs that were moving and walking. I would help certain people and get to know them. I needed to feel again. Feel useful and feel for others. There was a group of us, sadly a mix of paras and quads. They were great people, but their life had changed in a second, like mine. We bonded in the best way we could. Music and drugs. The guys' room was down the hall, and one of the nurses suggested that I should go and join the *party*. A visitor to one of the guys brought his guitar on Friday nights, and they usually had a jam session. The song that night was "Blowing in the Wind." I remember looking around and thinking sad thoughts. I was missing my crew of friends and the Friday nights we used to share. I tried singing and harmonizing with the rest, but it was difficult. At my introduction to the other kids, I remember saying, "Hi, I'm Laurie. I'm a quad, and this sucks." Claudia smiled, and I was "in."

It was an odd feeling, this new crew that I was now a part of with a tough initiation, a forever hazing. At night, some of us who were able to, were eager to explore our surroundings. Really, it was just any excuse to leave the floor. Our usual ride was to the cafeteria in NYU, as close to the closing time as possible. So, on a Friday or Saturday night, as you might have been getting yourselves ready for some party or new dance floor, five of us were getting ourselves ready for a big ride "late at night" to the grill. Let's just say that I needed my pectorals and shoulders to kick in because I could not wheel that damn chair, and no one cared! They rode way ahead of me, laughing the whole time, but it didn't matter! We ate crappy cheeseburgers, which tasted so much better than the ones that I never ate on the dinner tray. I do not remember if we ever paid for them—we must have seemed the most pitiful to the staff. It didn't matter, we were independent for a while, and loved it.

Another outing was a ride up to the roof. We were all convinced that we could feel a little better for a few hours if we indulged in the recreation type of drugs. The kind that friends thought would help take the edge off. People felt sorry for us. We didn't argue that. Since I was the only *standing* member of this group with hands and now legs that functioned, I was the appointed helper. I stood in a circle of around eight people, all in wheelchairs, and all with little or no hand or finger function. When I attempted to light a lighter and then pass the joint to the others, it was more than just pass. I had to hold it to their lips and see if they could take enough of a breath to even get anything out of it. Quads do not have good respiratory function until they gain strength or sometimes never. There were the laughable moments, like when I made several attempts to get a flame from a lighter. It's a tricky thing to maneuver the little screwy thing with your thumb and then quickly hold the other end to maintain the flame. I awkwardly had to use two hands. And we all counted the attempts, in unison, "One, two, three, four," and either laugh or cry when my thumb would slip or not be able to flick the Bic.

With great anticipation, my fellow roofers were hopeful, and after many trials and errors, we got fire! Finally, I shared a hit with everyone, one for them, one for me, one for them, two for me. Sometimes they were slow and didn't catch on. On one occasion, Chris wanted to hold it and asked me to put the joint in between his fingers. Let's just say that he had poor or no finger movements and it slipped onto Chris's lap! It was still smoking, and he started to scream, "Take it off my lap!" Well guess who was the only one capable to do this? This crazy stuff is what bonded us for the time. The craziness of just being eighteen, the craziness of being eighteen and in Quadternity.

SHE DID SAY, "YOU'RE GOING TO WALK"!!!

One hundred days post-accident. It is time. The most anticipated day, December 14! I was on the parallel bars. I was going to walk today in the physical therapy room. "Okay, Laurie, one foot at a time, lift your toes, heel strike, lift again on left side, repeat." It wasn't exactly a walk down the catwalk, but I did it, and I remember looking at Donna. She smiled and said, "Told ya!"

After my first day up and walking, I couldn't help thinking, "OH baby, it's going to be a while before I go home, a long while," but I was happy. I got back into what was my temporary wheelchair, and I rushed down to call my mom at work before she left to come visit, the usual highway, bridge, tunnel, and New York City traffic headache! Back to see me, like she did, every day for almost four and a half months at Rusk. I remember telling my mom on the phone, "I walked today, mom, I did, I just walked," and she cried happy tears, finally a momentous day! She screamed happy!

Walking this December was my Christmas gift! I spent the next nine days walking as much as possible before the big Christmas Eve holiday. Donna was encouraging me all the way. We became friends, to me this was a huge part of my recovery. I needed that support from someone who knew what I was up against. Our first major task for the real world: Find shoes I could wear!

My closet at home was full of heels, shoes with an average heel height of four inches or more. So, with this basic fashion need, what do two girls do? We went shopping! We found sneakers that were okay for then, for that purpose. I had to get used to compromise. My days of getting the latest trend, sadly, would have to be put on hold. Shopping for shoes now is still a horror. Walking in shoes is still a horror. If I find shoes that I feel good in, I buy few colors or even the same color, just—because. But how do I go back now into real life? It takes more than just putting a smile on your face. Uhm, someone had to get me out back into the world to socialize. I remember that day shopping for those shoes was my first time back in a store shopping. A bit overwhelming, especially at the cash register when I had to use a credit card. I felt slow and clumsy, and hating it as it went. I thought the cashier was screaming, "Come on slowpoke!" He wasn't—it was just in my mind.

We went to bars and restaurants and even took limo rides. Ha, ha, private joke, if you remember. I mean, I refer to this jokingly, but the reality of me "mingling in" with my crowd or any crowd was left to be known. This is unfamiliar territory. You become instantly aware of the world you "roll" in now, so to speak. You are now quite different; you're in the "handicapped" section. (This phrase is often used online for ticketing venues, so people in wheelchairs or other devices can be seated in the audience, but really? I think it is so exclusive!) Getting used to being in a "normal" environment or out in public spaces brought a whole other "getting used to" again. You're suddenly aware of steps, if there are any, into a restaurant or building. Or a door that you must open and quickly, somehow, get past or its weight will come back and hurt you. Then perhaps maneuvering on a slippery floor and some pulled out chairs to sweep around. Even holding a fork or dealing with certain foods that you avoid ordering because you cannot cut the steak or anything else with utensils. I always felt like the eyeballs were screaming, "Girl, what happened to you? Here goes clumsy and awkward." But most of my dear friends said it wasn't the cane or how I thought I looked odd. It was that they were staring at me because I'm cute, or something apologetic for the awkward way I felt. They are great friends. But how come I never hear that way of thinking? My self-thoughts are big negative.

Going to therapy was now exciting and hopeful. Some warm up exercises and again I was on the parallel bars. It felt good to stand up tall and do this! Getting up, vertical, yes, standing straight to walk upright again, was difficult, but I was young, and despite this trauma, I did it. I did get up and walk, and whatever technical failures I may now have, it's not perfect or the way I would have liked things to be, but I do walk, and I am so very thankful! This was a huge and important detail if I was going to be able to go home on Christmas holiday. It would be a real test to see if I could adjust back to an independent life. When you get up in the morning, go downstairs for your breakfast. Clean up the kitchen, and then go back upstairs to shower and get dressed for the day. Whew. All that in Rusk was important. Just learning how to get out of bed was huge. I was not yet walking without a device of some sort. In fact, I needed the wheelchair when I needed to use the bathroom and go to all my therapy. It was only when I was close to the end of my inpatient care that I used two canes to walk. Eventually, I learned to use just one cane in outpatient care, a year later.

Back to that funny game the insurance companies play. Well, it was in 1979. Some companies understand that you want to go home to celebrate at home with family and friends, and then return to the rehab facility. Some companies aren't great; they play games with your emotions and threaten to drop your coverage if you're not in the facility twenty-four hours! They do not want to pay for you to be gallivanting around town, but not on Christmas, just not on Christmas.

I wasn't sure how it would go anyway. My mom's house in Brooklyn had six exterior steps to get in the house, and my bedroom was upstairs, fourteen steps upstairs. Climbing at that time was asking a lot for me to do. I had to flex (bring up) my hip flexors to raise my foot to put it on a step and then do the same with the other leg and foot. And then also lift my other leg with my arm, and the cane, and where do I put that in this scenario? It was difficult, but I did it, I did one step at a time, and I did whatever it took to reach the inside of my home. My home, my familiarity, it was this that I missed, and running up those stairs so many times before.

My biggest enemy was not the height of the staircase or the task before me. It was often that voice of defeat that sang to me. The problem was that I tried to do walking as I did walking before. That, well, just wasn't there. Not being where? That's the NEURO line, the one that glows and screams, "YOU HAD A SPINAL CORD INJURY AND YOU WILL NEVER BE "NORMAL" AGAIN!!!"

What does this mean? I had a demanding time with this reality at some point. I mean, what's the sense of trying to walk if I am not going to walk like I wanted to? You know, glide down the street, in your fabulous coat and just, float, or move freely without the mental coaching for every step.

I was mad and angry and often thought, "Hey, you, able-bodied person, who never had a spinal cord injury, you don't have to think of placing your toes or foot in the correct position. You're not thinking,

53

"I hope I lift my foot enough so that I won't fall." I always must consider flooring underneath me, this is crazy—oh, and at the same time, I am also trying to lift my head when I walk.

My thoughts also included complaints of my new differences. I became very aware of my circumstances at all times and I did hate that I had to *think* so much, just to walk across the room. Maneuver, a great word to look up in Dictionary.com: *to skillfully change or be adroitness*. I like adroitness, I am an Adroit! I have been skillfully maneuvering this body and mind for thirty-eight years.

In therapy, they would be telling me that to try to lift my head and walk at the same time was like rubbing your head and rubbing the tummy at same time kind of thing. Also, having to pee and walk at same time is difficult in case anyone asked. I guess it's a brain-to-nerve and muscle thing. I used to say, "Come on, body, work together on this." I may have referred to this before, but it wasn't so crazy after all. As part of a new trend in the "workout" world, trainers and coaches are using terms like brain to engage, concentrate on the body part, and get a connection to it. It's a mental thing. Well, I have been doing my version of the *brain to gain* thing for a long time now. It just came natural to me. It's like making a phone call to a certain phone number but the lines get crossed and your signal jumps to another muscle group or unknown area and it may work or it may not. So, you try.

"How pathetic and simple my goals are now," I used to think. I was eighteen and had to concentrate on what was before me now! This was more than a tough pill to swallow. Okay, forget the fabulous coat, the groove, the float, the guys. For my new walk or swagger, I need to figure out how to stop my toes from gripping the ground or how to walk when my toes freeze up, which makes my foot spasm into an ankle spasm, up the calf and up higher. It's like you have tiny hands and fingers inside your toes and legs pulling in the opposite direction that you're trying to move in, and then literally walk. So, what are my options? Wheelchair? Does this mean I gave up in my efforts to walk again? Or is it failure, or is this the safe choice? I cannot honestly remember deciding. It was so exciting that I was walking, with all the imbalances in muscle strength and innervations (nerves getting the message) and the weakness.

I was at least up and getting stronger every day that I moved. I can remember trying to button a button, to put it through the tiny receiving hole on the other side of the blouse, to grasp it enough to carry out this task. This took months. It wasn't so much the button being done but the *need to do*. The need to do whatever I could do using whatever muscles and movement that were cooperating at the time. Just me walking without thinking, now there is novel idea. It sounds nonsensical and weird to describe this, but hey, they are my dreams. I can still use my mind freely, can't I? Sometimes I cannot. The war in me is charted between before and after; my whole life is now on a timeline. Pre-accident or post-accident. Pre- September 4, 1979, or post-. Everything now is factored off that date. It's a standard. It's my cutoff date, my life, as I knew it. I was young. Eighteen, and now I have a timeline of heavy presence. Can I survive this? Will I be able to live a life like this, do I want to? Depression is horrible. A ghost of taunting. Voices in your mind so loud that your conversations with yourself are a routine now, a new reality. My voices were mean, loud, full of self-hate. I was full of doubt. Full of fear of the what if, of the *why me*. I hate this life. I hate this constant on. Please shut it off. I do confess I know this all sounds so irresponsible of me. So full of self-hate, self-disgust. Well, it was. I had all that.

The days were long and tiring in rehab, at least for me. I was usually on the mats at nine a.m., learning how to roll over. I had an unusual method, Donna said. I used my head to pivot first. I remember demonstrating this, for the other PTs. The move was first the head and then the body spin. We also did a lot of leg strengthening, trying to wake up and strengthen my quadriceps, hamstrings, abductors, adductors, glutes, anything down the leg. Any sign of muscle strength and we were on it. I was crawling, then up on my knees, to up standing. We did a lot more than that. A lot of balancing work, to get my trunk stable. It was a process, a difficult one, but it was working! Too bad we didn't film it; it would make a great routine for other SCIs who are in this type of rehab.

My physical therapy was straight or broken up with occupational therapy. I never called it occupational therapy—it was just "hands" to me. The goals were to get my fingers to work, to straighten out, to be functional. My left hand still has all the fingers in a permanent bent fixture. Occupational therapy was important for many reasons. My right hand works at about 90% functional. My fingers are straighter, and I can do more intricate tasks with it. O.T. is useful to get hands and mind moving, and they do this with puzzles, art, and various forms of expression. I remember painting and drawing there a lot, and frequently getting fitted for hand braces, my famous VELCRO©-tape nightmares at two a.m. when I had to pee.

At some point, I insisted on getting up, no matter how many times a night, to pee. I was ready, willing and able, and it was a great achievement and thrill to escape the catheter. In therapy, everyone is looking to get well, to improve. There's a lot of hope, but it doesn't come to everyone. I felt guilty. It was the PT room, it seemed so large and important. A double-door entry into a large space. A room of new hope for some, or a real hatred for the movements of torture that some patients were experiencing. My friend, who had ALS (Lou Gehrig's disease), a motor neuron disease, screamed through every stretching session he had. The parallel bars were the first thing you saw as you entered, and there were other large areas of mats, elevated at "seat" level so that wheelchair transfers were achievable. So, all these people, if I may borrow a phrase, wounded warriors, were trying to feel or move a toe for the first time, or anything. They were also watching and waiting that day. I remember feeling survivor's guilt, as they call it. I was thinking, "This sucks." First, I dreamed of walking again, all this time doing the *why me* chant? Why did this happen? Now I feel guilty that I'm doing this, I'm walking!

"OK, Laurie, remember to get those glutes working and quads and hamstrings fired!" Donna said often with a smile. I did manage to learn a lot of body parts and anatomy lessons fluently. I got up from the wheelchair, every day now, it was my favorite part of my day. Donna was ready, the PT assistant was ready, it's showtime! As I previously mentioned, the steps were carefully planned, and I hoped that I could execute them. I did this walk and spent hours in the parallel bars going back and forth learning my new skills.

Yes! yes, I am on my way! My dreams are coming true, I'm hopeful to walk out of Rusk! Well, I did, in June of 1980. That is, seven months and eighteen days later in Rusk, plus the two months in St. Vincent's, almost one year. Wow, sometimes it feels like I could remember every day, every conversation. Sometimes I wish I didn't, it's harmful to remember bad memories. They are haunting. I often wake up frightfully to see a team of doctors in their white lab coats standing around my bed, checking their notes about me, staring. I have issues with people staring at me. Still do.

Walking was exciting, new and different. A new skill set I needed for this: patience! Let's face it, if there is a possibility to walk, even if it's not perfect or "normal," you're going to take it. Especially when you are given a new hope! Especially, when on day number one of real rehab, your PT says, "You're going to walk!" I was doing this, I was putting my best foot forward, and the fact that I was walking, with all the imbalances in muscle strength and slight innervation (nerves that are getting the message) and all the other body weaknesses, was amazing at this point in my rehab. It was 100 days post-accident! That is three months and ten days later! I was up and getting stronger. I had to get stronger, "It was all going to take time," said this new voice, this new hope was now in this boxing ring. I had a new chant, "This quad walks!"

FOREVER IS A LONG TIME

If you're a new SCI person, I would love to offer you some advice. Do not accept any statement from a *whitey* (doctor in a white lab coat). From the very first hour of my injury, I overheard the E.M.T say, "Spinal cord injury, a shame, she may not ever walk again." Then the ER doctors said a similar thing: "Paralysis, slim chance of walking."

And the St. Vincent's staff or resident neurosurgeon said to me and my mom, right before surgery, "You will never walk again, this surgery will only stabilize your neck at the point of injury." His name was Doctor Ho. Why did I remember his name so clearly? Well first, he was the doctor who STRUCK FIRST WITH A NO-HOPE AGENDA with his words. He officially took away any hope of recovery, a recovery we were hoping for at that time, which was, "When would I be walking?"

It's the first question that comes to mind, which comes so piercing into your brain that it floods the thought process of anything else. A consuming and screaming need to know, "Will I ever regain use of my body!" The basic desire only to walk again. To rise from "zero," my reference of nothing. Deadness as in no feeling or to feel a toe, and then nine more. To feel your feet and the toes attached. The top of your foot, the bottom of your foot, the ankle, the calf, up the leg, jeez, I'm so intense, some people say, when I describe this process. Well, FYI, when you're newly dead, when you feel nothing below your chest area, each new feel is a victory. Each twitter of muscle, or nerve, each touch to feel, is detailed in your mind and sensory awareness. I had to concentrate on the very *presence* of each toe and all the other body parts I just described. It's exhausting and it's lonely. Because no one, and I do mean no one, understands this.

Oh, that doctor who said I will never walk again? He comes back into my life again. One Saturday night, while sitting in the hallway at Rusk, I heard his name being paged over the loudspeaker (Rusk was physically connected to NYU Hospital). "Doctor Ho, Doctor, please report to nurse's station." Uh, is this the same doctor, just a few months earlier, the doctor who leveled me with a sentence of hopelessness? At once, I went down to my nurse's station and asked her to get in touch with him and asked that he come see me. I was anxious to see him, I planned the whole event. I kept asking myself, okay, now what am I going to say? Am I going to scream at him for being so definite, the last time I saw him, about the fact that I would never regain use of my body? I thought how great it would be if I stood up and walked to him. I'll show him to not take away anyone's hope ever again!

At the last minute, I panicked. I thought, "Laurie you are crazy, you are going to confront this man, he's a neurosurgeon after all. This is nuts." I kept the room dark. He walked in and asked who requested to see him. I was the only one in the room as he zeroed in on my face, but he still had no clue who I was. I guess my physical transformation had begun and I had changed so much that he really didn't recognize me. I stood up and took a few steps. I could tell by his face that he honestly had no idea, and why he was there.

My voice quivered, but I said, "You told me in September, in St. Vincent's Hospital, the night before my surgery, that I would never walk again. You told me I would have to get used to life in a wheelchair, forever, and that I needed to come to terms with this." The light came on, not the lamp by my bed, but he now remembered! He frowned and sincerely apologized and said, "It's just that so many do not do as well as you. I had to tell you that, you are lucky, you got your miracle." I cried after he left, not only for me, but because it is true that so many spinal cord injured people do not walk again ever. Forever is a long time.

ADVICE FROM ME

Ok, SCI person, so you may feel that you're diagnosed with this "death sentence." If I may, at least I felt that way for a while. Some people may find this wording difficult. But the person that you were and knew and loved, that person is dead. Oh, don't worry, you will eventually deal with the new you. Your soul, your person, your being, the person inside that you were, will eventually come out. It may take a long time to bring that inner person back. It's up to you, and you have a choice at some point. You need to mourn and then go on with a new life. Your grieving process is like losing a loved one in the real sense of death. The process is difficult, exhausting and forever. I do not think you will ever get to the point of total escape from that memory of your old self. If this is your situation, it only dims or lessens in the madness. It's true that we are we all afraid to say things as such. Why do I have to hide my feelings and push them to the side or leave those emotions in the past? I am angry. This isn't fun, and the brave victor and strong person that I need to be? She doesn't always show up. I need to deal with that, I need to deal with a new life and all the baggage of my old one. I am still inside. I am, but I can't be that person anymore. I must transform and be changed. I do not want this, but, as I said before, I have to figure out this life now. Living it the hard way. It true, it's real. This would be the mature way of thinking this out. The *I learned it the hard way* type.

That doctor was not the first or last to make "himself perfectly clear." They usually go by statistics. Some doctors with whom I spoken frankly with do believe in "the man upstairs" or "God," but how many SCI patients regain use of their body? How many walk again? These were my questions. I wanted to know, are there others like me? Now that I am being discharged, what do I do now? Also, in 1979, the research was in its very unthinkable stage—to imagine that a spinal cord injured person could ever walk with the help of a device or through the miracle of surgery for complete recovery! A great vision, it was the beginning. It is happening now! There are now designs for exoskeleton robotic devices that could take people out of their wheelchairs! This is so exciting, and the researchers are making these devices so streamlined that they can be like leggings or stockings that are hardwired to make you move! Oh, the joy this will bring to three million plus SCI people! And this can apply to so many other mobility issues that people have. This is so needed for the aging public, who by age alone have mobility and walking issues. Can you imagine, people will rise from their chairs and beds and walk!

By the time this becomes mainstream, it will be normal in our eyes to see robotic devices, and we will become part of the norm. And who would imagine that during the process and development of such devices for a physical need, that they will lead technology into a full robotic world! I'm excited, I definitely want one like Rosie the robot in the Jetsons cartoon!

GOING HOME

Be Careful What You Ask For

"Laurie, you're able to go home now!" Wow, the words I waited to hear, for the last seven or eight long months in Rusk, and the first two months in St. Vincent's. It has been almost one year of hospital life. I hoped for this day and well, here it is. Tomorrow I will leave this New York City address and go home, to my house in Brooklyn.

The plan was that I go home but come back for outpatient therapy three times a week. Donna *somehow* managed to get transferred as well! She later told me, "I was not going to let you out of my sight. We worked too hard." Thank God, I felt better to keep working with her. I didn't want to work with a new therapist and learn his or her new tricks. Donna knew me, from day one.

We worked on my gait and other balance techniques. Hey, I remember working with those large stability balls, way before the big craze. In fact, in therapy we worked on floor techniques and other foundational mat therapy, which is so similar to Pilates mat work that I do now.

With the great news of going home, I had to prepare, not only physically, but also mentally, for the worst of times. I needed to get paperwork from an office on the main floor of NYU, so I went downstairs in a wheelchair to help get it expedited. Did I say I had to prepare mentally?

In the late afternoon, the lobby was busy with visitors, doctors, nurses, therapists, all changing shifts, coming in or going home. I hurried into a crowded elevator and a man helped me move over to the side. I was sitting and felt eyes staring at me. It was not a child, but a little person, a dwarf. And not only was that uncomfortable, but I knew her eyes. I glanced over through the suits and raincoats, to a pair of shoes that I recognized standing next to her. Her older brother! I dated this guy, it was only last year and now if he notices me, OMG! He was the guy I met walking on my way to school one morning. We had the same swagger and the same long wool wrap winter coat. Mine was dark green and his was camel, golden like his hair. It was windy and we both were walking with the collar pulled up high around our cheeks. He noticed this and followed me onto the bus. I never made it to class that day. We got off the next stop and walked for hours arm and arm in our coats in the cold together. It must be true, I look so different now. The transformation and change that my body was going through was still in process. I still was unrecognizable. Only I did not realize how much! The elevator stopped and they both were getting off. He turned and looked! He looked right at me and did not recognize me at all. Maybe, I like to think, maybe he did and wanted to be polite. Maybe he did and was horrified, thinking to himself, wow, she's messed up Now again, what are the chances… I must look horrible; the real world is definitely going to be rough. I was being prepared physically for the change but mentally I needed more time. When I got back upstairs to my room, I looked in the mirror and thought, "Wow, it's been nine months, almost a year, since you even thought about makeup." I had forgotten what it was like to get excited to get dressed and get myself ready for a great day. I had forgotten what it was like to even care.

THRILLS OF ANOTHER KIND

I was frightened, ashamed and proud at the same time. How can that be? I was afraid of my future and the mighty dilemma in front of me. Only we did not speak about it. We did not *explore* or speak about the hurtful things or events that just happened, the type of hurts that are so big that it feels like yesterday; the pain is still so real and intimate, so touchable. How come? Why do all the shitty things in life, the heartaches, the traumas, why do they shock us and linger in the front of all our other memories so vividly? Why is their detail so 4-K clear that they are usually detailed, bit by bit? So sharp and bright that they somehow dim the happy and joyful memories.

I was embarrassed because I could not believe the physical change and permanent change that my eyes were adjusting to. At the tender age of eighteen, the demands for a hot body were bad enough, that type of image or woman that we conform to admittingly or not from Hollywood, fashion mags and ourselves. Oh, girl, get that perfect selfie and lip pout! But for me, this new physical demand was the survivor type in the real sense. Hello. reality TV, I'll take a damn year on a remote island any day to forgo this realness. I know many people who should be getting a million dollars, who are survivors of this life! I can show you the real drama of a survival competition, the drama, against yourself. The type that takes an everyday resilience in everyday circumstances. So, let me resist any further unpleasantries to the phony toughies on those phony television reality-challenging survival escapades.

Everyone kept saying, "Be proud of yourself!" Right now, I needed to learn a healthy pride. How now to be proud, a pride enough that I can walk again. You think it would be easy! I had to retrain my mind to rethink. I began reading about athletes and what they do to motivate themselves. And with every step I took, it was as if I would hear the famous "Wide World of Sports" intro line, "The thrill of victory!" And I had to get past the *it's not like you were before* voice because I am walking again! I am doing what the doctors said I would not ever do. I am vertical and still walking every day for the last thirty-eight years. That's survivor skills. I survived death and drowning. I survived the first twenty-four hours, I survived spinal fusion surgery, twice! I survived the Halo, and nurse Marianne. I walked one hundred days after the injury and managed to climb those *thrill of victory* steps up into my neighbor's home that New Year's Eve with three seconds to spare!

I was now seeing the progress that was a result of all the effort, and it was paying off. Therapy was hopeful, and I was really thinking I could do this new life. I can, with a lot of *work and patience sprinkled in*. Would it be this same kind of curriculum for the next few months? Six months? A year? Disciplines of being consistent, picking up my chin when it hurts and wiping away tears until? Reality check again! I was in this for life, kid, get used to it. I had to self-talk myself so much. This was a human drama of athletic competition of a whole new kind. My thrills of another kind. The winner's podium was still far off, but I was in the race, I was putting myself in these games, these serious games of my new life.

SEE'YA!

The day came, and I said my goodbyes. I had met some wonderful doctors, nurses and especially physical and occupational therapists. It was bitter sweet, but not too bad, because I was coming back in a few days and I could see them again and share my home and new walking war stories with them.

I remember waiting for my mom to get the car and pull it up on the circular driveway at Rusk, so I could easily get in. I remember the fresh air hitting my face, and I thought, "The wind feels good, just don't blow me down." It has happened, trust me, my enemies are not normal. Funny thing, the chilly wind made us rush inside on my first day at Rusk, back in November. Now, in my day of departure, this new wind was a refreshing reminder that I could be enjoying it! I can be back outside in the sun! I remember crying tears of fear, because in the hospital world, I was "the successful one." I remember my psychologist saying, "In here, in the hospital world, you did great." Now I was re-entering the real world, where I am not the star, I am not successful. I am at the other end of the spectrum, I am now a disabled person and will be and will enter a whole new world.

My mom prepared the house for me as best as she could, but my bed was now in the living room! The fourteen steps up to my bedroom were not going anywhere, so I had to hurry up and get stronger and learn how to get up that staircase because the living room was not going to cut it forever. And there were hospital gadgets all over the house. Plastic bed pans, chucks, a wheelchair, a walker, crutches and those socks with the sticky rubber bottoms. This bedroom-room replacement was not what I was dreaming about.

I guess you can say my house wasn't accessible or independent-friendly. I did have to adjust, here at home, everything was difficult. Independent living was going to be a new kind of living. Independent had a whole new meaning. Can I be alone while my mom was at work? Can I fix breakfast or lunch, and could I even get to the kitchen? Thankfully, there was a bathroom on the main level. A very big deal.

Ahhh, the pie-in-your-face reality was so overwhelming. At Rusk, they kept telling me, "The reason we are stalling is because you need to learn how to be independent! This doesn't mean you are capable of normal independence, like working, school, driving, dating, shopping, banking, all the normal things young people do at nineteen." Independent for me and SCI people meant getting to the bathroom by yourself. Take a shower with or without a shower chair, stand up now! (Although I think we bought a shower chair and I used it for a long while.)

Dress yourself. Yes, it was still a struggle to get socks on. (Forget about hosiery, I still cannot do them.) Um, let's see, *is it the independence* to then go downstairs, cook and eat breakfast all by yourself? The list is tiring, and we didn't even get to lunch yet. Days at home now were long and filled with so much frustration, and my dream to go home turned into a nightmare of torment. How am I going to live like this? And how about going out? Going to the store? Again, I knew that it was going to be a hard life. I was not on a general campaign of complaining. It was the adjustment, the anticipation and buildup of feeling warm and fuzzy at home that I longed for. I had to learn to see my glass half-full, I had to remember where I just came from. I had to remember that I had a new independent. *Could do*, that had to replace *can't*! I had to learn how to make *I can* literally come out of my mouth. I would say it over and over again out loud. The front door was a scary place for me. So many mornings I would go to the door, put my hand on the doorknob to open it, but didn't. I had panic attacks. On a good day I was able to do the *I Can-* my inner thoughts were coaching me minute by minute. Once I got down the front stairs, I walked carefully up to the corner, past some onlookers (neighbors) who knew me. Neighbors who saw me so many times before running up to the corner to catch the train or bus. They knew I was the girl who had the terrible accident. They knew but just weren't sure. They weren't sure if they should ask me what happened. They weren't sure if they should say hello. It began, the starring and awkwardness. So annoying people can be, I was trying to do my lift - the -foot, self -talk song, and now I have to add this element to the craziness.

COPING AND ATTITUDE

Since early on in this new life search for normalcy, and in a search for what the heck do I do now, I tried ridiculously hard to remove myself from anything related to the word "handicapped." I wanted to return to my old self! I kept going back and forth and comparing, such a dangerous place to be. In my delusion of this endeavor, I ran from and desperately figured out how to do whatever it took to get back to the very life I thought I deserved. Does this make sense? I do not know what kept me going or motivated, it must have been youth and the incredible hope that just maybe, I could get this body to near normal, whatever that meant.

While waiting in my doctor's office, flipping through some fashion magazine, I saw pictures of women working out, thinking that this would have been me, that's who I was. Again, comparing old me versus the new me. Some self-talk actually worked! Those I had to work on. Those positive self-talks needed the most rehab at this time. Unfortunately, most of my self-talks sounded like this: "So now I must identify as someone else. Someone else I don't really like, someone I'm not sure that I know. She is new, but really the same ole me, but different. I'm terrified, this body is shaky, I don't know if I can translate the struggle, the physical barrier, the internal barriers, what the heck is going on inside my body, is this right? Do I dare walk like this?"

I had to ask myself these questions so often, so often that I could not relate to anyone. I may have looked like I was *okay*, and adjusted, but inside I sometimes couldn't breathe around people, around "normal" people. Ugh, you see I think the comparison of normal to not-normal comes from you all. Ha, me too, sometimes, I admit. "Different" people, you know, the obvious: the wheelchair person, the cane walker, the amputee, the Down Syndrome or CP person, the person who has obvious physical differences. When I joined this group of peoples, I soon learned that I was in another dimension, almost. Barriers that go beyond the physical, which is hard enough, but barriers of reactions and emotions that were so challenging. I was not ready to handle this. In my anger, what helped me to cope was when I used the "f- you" momentum sometimes. It is the attitude of f-you, don't look at me funny or treat me oddly. I must get up, go to school and do "normal" again, only do this now, in this body. Leave me alone, stop staring and give me a break.

Then there also another coping attitude of "I'm okay, really, I am going to bite my lip, keep my chin up high and smile, blah blah blah." It works for a while, somehow, the f-you mode just feels better to say sometimes. I was young, I was hurt. I was two people sliding from anger to hope, constantly. The hurt person always wanted to be well, free from the pain. I was hurt and needed to feel justified in that. It was depressing, it was painful, traumatic and life-changing. But, oddly enough, this all led me to the hopeful and determined me! Constant bouts of "No, I can't!" at the same time led me to "Oh yes, you can, it's just that you have to know it's going to be different, it's going to be scary." My conversations with myself were classic, and I wish I'd recorded them!

Some other conversations I have with people is always interesting and have always managed to make me scratch my head. I would internalize and evaluate whether this would be a good or bad conversation and oftentimes laugh out loud. Especially the conversation that went like this..."Oh yeah, I know what you're going through, it's tough. Last year I broke my wrist and couldn't do anything for ten weeks. I couldn't shower the way I like to, and I couldn't even dress myself."

Also, the conversation with the person who somehow feels the need to "top" me. They feel that they can identify so much with me and that their trauma or their illness has a competition element to it. Now, please let me be clear, I have total respect for fellow sufferers in pain and faced with either a fatal illness or a no-answer or no-cure situation. I can relate and honestly can say that I would never imply anything else.

I have learned that my questions and reactions to those types of peoples that I have mentioned are usually laughable. I smile now as they share. I choose no longer to be in that arena with them. I used to become very defensive of myself. *How dare you compare your situation to mine. You have no clue what spinal cord injury is like unless you have personally been connected to this nightmare. And I can tell as soon you explain and give me your knowledge of such medical intellect (insert eye roll emoji HERE, please)!*

So, my fellow sufferer, survivor, and those *dealing* with the journey, be prepared. Guard your heart, keep your focus and move on. Save your breath for real.

CATCHING UP

Going to college was such a great decision. It was an enormous next step. Literally *now doing and living the real world of normal.* I often wondered, "What was next for my normal chain, college, career, marriage etc.? Was this possible for me?" It was crazy, and I think of it now and wonder how I did those things. I wish I had realized my accomplishments at that time, because what I did on that first day of college was more than I had done physically for months. I put myself in "normal," I put myself in "you're going to do this." I do so appreciate all this now, because I am seeing big accomplishments, for what I did in such a short amount of time, post-accident.

As another new school year approached, Tamar, my vocational counselor, suggested community college, just so I would not be so far behind, and it would be good to get out and be amongst my peers. PEERS? Ha, well we might have been the same age, but we were NOT peers at all in my world. I attended a local community college in Brooklyn. It was by the ocean, which was great in warm months, but those ocean breezes made my already unsteady walk even harder to push this body through. Wind was my enemy! I had to secretly pray, "Lord, please don't let me get knocked over."

Humility should have been my first name, as it became *my* common. And I had to learn how to be this way. I was so humiliated at times—talk about walking and talking amongst my *peers?* It didn't seem possible to even hurt or cry more than I had already cried. These kids, people my age, their biggest concern at this stage in their life was meaningless to me. They didn't have to worry about wind, that they may lose bladder or bowel control, or how to maneuver their cane, bookbag and walk at the same time. We weren't even on the same page.

It was a new era, the 1980's. I lost some time, I didn't keep up with the current news, or music or television world. I had my own TV drama to live out. I had changed so much. But here, this crowd seemed to be locked in a time warp. I was bored here; this wasn't a place of great learning, and not that I was a gifted student, but when the cafeteria was the place to *be* and show off your new Gloria Vanderbilt or Jordache jeans and hear some escapades of their weekends? Same old, same old. I had to move on, I needed more. I felt that I couldn't relate anymore to their silliness, I felt like I had been through a war and returned to what was once normal. It isn't anymore, it will never be. I remember the tragic morning after John Lennon was shot. I was on campus, it was December 8, 1980. This means I was back to "normal" life in one year, fifteen months, after my tragic day. I am amazed I did that. Looks like the *I could* is pushing out the *I can't*. Well, for now. Small victories, they add up to big ones. It's true, if you genuinely want to change something, you must start somewhere. I did, even in all this confusion and the impossible knowledge that "things" would get better. *I claimed Hope for my determination. I pushed for the hope, the hope that I would continually improve.* Let's tally one up for good self- talk and being hopeful!

WITH OR WITHOUT

Later that semester I applied to University of Florida's School of Journalism. I got accepted, it was college road trip time! I really liked warm Florida, and oh, how nice it would be to go to school with shorts on every day. But this University of Florida, aka, Gator country, was out in the sticks, and for a city girl, that was a stretch, not sure if I could relate.

Seemed nice, bell tower, a traditional feel on campus, but large. Exceptionally large. The admissions director smartly pointed out to me that the campus is so huge that "kids with no problems" had a challenging time getting around, and they had to take buses to various schools on campus, as far as thirty minutes across.

"Kids with no problems." Geez, I guess I "have problems." I got stuck on those words. I knew what she meant, and it wasn't the first time I'd heard that, or even casually put, but when people genuinely didn't notice, I always noticed, a bit too much. Why do I have so many hang-ups? Dear University of Florida School of Journalism, thanks for the admission, but you're too much to tackle right now.

Okay, I'll stay in New York, closer to home. Fashion Institute of Technology was the obvious choice; it was only one city block. I could handle this campus. Four buildings to maneuver and easy access. Wow, this was fun, and it was real college, no snobby business fake-like fashion school, as in my original plan, and it was part of the SUNY school system. Tamar, my counselor, became a "friend" as well. She believed in me, so much that she went with me into the admissions director's office and asked them to give me a chance. She told them that *I can handle this* and that *one day they will be proud of me*.

My first giant of challenges, amongst many more to come. Usually, I did not shy away from challenges. I like to think I just did whatever it took. I was still dreaming, still wanting to do something great with my life.

I had no choice as soon as I stepped out, into my life at college in New York. I put myself right in the big city and dared myself everyday into a new life. I had difficulties beyond comprehension at times. It was all new, all difficult, and I was meeting new people every day. It wasn't "if" someone asks me why I used a cane, it was "when." With every new person I met, I had a new struggle to deal with. Telling "my story" was another change to adapt to and most endeavors with this crowd had to include my story.

People wanted to know! They wanted to know why someone so young walks with a cane. It seemed like I had a sign on my forehead that said, "Ask me," and it should have included, "at your own risk." It was funny that an *average* person was rare at FIT. Most kids were a little *out there* on the edge in one way or another. Sexually, artistically, these kids were definitely more than just fashion junkies. Punk rock was hot, boys with painted fingernails and hair was high and molded. And then there was me. I guess I may have thought I stuck out because I used a cane, but when I think about it, I fit right in. I loved being with them, I felt normal in that crowd.

"Optimism is the faith that leads to achievement. Nothing can be done without hope and confidence."

— Helen Keller

I did stop and ask myself, "Am I crazy to think I can do this, go to *away* college, and live on my own?" First night in a dorm alone, and I was trying to fit in. I had dreams, but this is ridiculous, everyone is eighteen and so young. I was twenty, and two Septembers after the accident, I was feeling so mature, but scarred. "Okay, girls, I used to say, "this is nothing, this is fun stuff, and you're so incredibly lucky to have reached eighteen, nineteen, or twenty without any scars. Me, I am done. Not too much can happen that's any worse than what I just got over." — Over? Did I just say this? It was really more like, "It's only just begun."

"Let's live," the girls on my dorm floor chanted every Friday night, sometimes every Thursday, Saturday, Sunday. Too many times. Yes, this is New York City, and there was Studio 54, Columbia University mixes, and the NYU frat boys. FIT girls are invited to lots of parties. I went, they were crazy times, the beginning of things I did in this new body. I had anger, and I had to get back a life, a life I thought I had missed out on.

It's a process, a humbling one. Getting knocked off a horse has consequences. It hurts because it is such a great fall, and I managed to keep falling off many times. I put myself in odd or bad situations "for a girl like me." I also wanted to stay on the edge of life, well, edgy for me, that's always a relative side of measuring. I think, typical story in my life. I thought I was entitled to do everything that everyone else was doing. That also included bad-girl behavior, just like everyone else. Like dancing in Studio 54 on Thursday nights, or climbing that big staircase and hanging out in that balcony lounge. I think I liked daring. That night it was Halloween, and I had met a guy in Brooklyn at a party and left early with him. I had a private VIP invite for FIT girls. I don't remember my costume or if I had one on, but the guy, the guy who was ecstatic just to get into 54 because he could never get past the bouncers at the door? He was thrilled. "What the heck? What am I doing with this total stranger I met only two hours earlier, brought him to New York, and lounging with him and he pulls out a mask with horns on it?" He was the Devil! I had the chills. A bad move on his part. I got up, left him there, hurried down the stairs, got in a cab and went back to my apartment. How did I do that????

At that point, if it was a challenge or a dare, I was still in for it. I was a traumatized young mind, thinking I was really all grown up, even still, "in spite of," all this sadness, I did have fun. I just wanted the comparison to stop, and I was trying to find myself both emotionally and physically. I also had to find a rhythm in walking, if that makes any sense to anyone. I am sure that if you have another kind of trauma or physical challenge that you deal with, there are the same emotional issues of returning to your life and then inventing a new one, dealing with the trauma and then moving on because sometimes there is not an answer. I kept searching for the answer...why the hell did this happen? Why was it allowed? No answer. So? (Lemonade, anyone?)

My days at school were also challenging because twelve credits were the least I could do per semester. It wasn't the academic challenge, just the entirety of it all. This was my first semester and first time I was away from my mom, family, friends, therapists, truly on my own. Getting up in the morning to shower in the dorms was rough for me; carrying myself, my towels, shampoo and other toiletries was an accomplishment all on its own. Also, I could hardly get dinner from the cafeteria all on my tray and get back to a table to eat! This is embarrassing. Yes, people helped. I went to dinner with roommates and friends, but the independent thing was subject to everything, every part of my day and night. Independence in specific things. I kept doubting if I could I really do this *on my own* thing. Like walking and chewing gum at the same time, only I had to worry about peeing. Worry about pooping! Check to see where the nearest bathroom was, carry books, grocery items, just running to the corner for something on my own, OMG! Here we go again, the record is on, the tapes, the negative vibes, they are all screaming, "This sucks!" Here we go again, this isn't fun, but I faked it as much as possible! Hello, coping strategies, where are you? I could do things, I could do normal-life things. I could go to school, study, graduate, and get a career, what other twenty-year-olds were doing. The *I could do everything just like I used to* chant was not working!

That was the part that I dreaded. Those were the tough times that Tamar discussed with me. The part where you know, but only when you go through it, when the sweat starts at your neck and you really need to hold tight the tears. Hold tight onto all the "good" thoughts people have for you. Hold tight to the prayers people have for you. Hold tight to every single positive message of fortitude and mental toughness that you can. My new beginning was challenging every second. And I talked to myself, I counted steps, I did wonder, "Does anyone hear me doing this? OMG, I think I am crazy! OMG, they probably think I am crazy!"

"Hello, people." I wanted to use a megaphone in the streets and scream. *Please remember my reality, walking was new. I used to be paralyzed, does anyone know what I am going through?? I am genuinely walking again! Does anyone understand this?* Silence.

I struggled with this blindness, the deafness of my success, even though I wanted more. I remembered what they told me at Rusk, "In here, at Rusk, you beat the odds, you're doing great, you're a star! But once you leave, you're out in the real world, you're a small fish." Talk about small fish—I'm a feeder fish!

I felt it, that exact smallness. Maybe because I still used a cane, maybe that's why I felt like my achievements wasn't appreciated. It wasn't enough that I took my first steps from being a quadriplegic, three months and ten days later! These people, these ordinary people, they don't get it. They just don't know! I felt like they were waiting for me to walk without the cane or even run. Then I would have a story, then I would be a success.

What they don't understand is the gap. The neuro gap, how wide and deep that is, the space that extends only to a dead end. Neurologically, there is a splice in my wires. It cannot reconnect. There is only so far that I can take this body. There is only so far that I can push it. If being back to normal, just as before, just like it never happened, is the expectation, then I will fail. But if the outlook is look where you've come from, look what you have accomplished, then I will enter that race. It's the only race that I win. I cannot compete with my old self, the expected self, the desired self, it's too unattainable. I wasn't quitting my hope and efforts to improve, but I did have to fight the dream to be physically normal just as before; this will defeat me every time. I must remember this and feel satisfied with small wins. How small is up to me. But they add up and then I can see the results. I need to go to the racetrack. Not to gamble but to check out some "blinders," like the horses wear to keep them focused, their eyes toward the finish line. I love this, there could be so many things going on around us to distract us. But when you're determined to win, and your goals are realistic, and you add in some prayers and some cheering on from your family and friends, you never know what can happen! Sounds good, this is the self-talk that needs to be on auto loop!

WALK THE TALK AND THEN SOME

My positive self-talk did have its moments of success. I had made huge progress with a single cane, and I surprise even myself in many ways. Usually, you could have found me walking and shopping in the West Village, either alone or with roommates. It wasn't unusual for me to walk from Washington Square Park up to Sixth Avenue to catch the bus, so, I can go up to Twenty-Seventh and then walk another long block up to my apartment at school. A mere "walk in the park" for most! After two years of rehab, learning about my body was an education.

Here we go again, I was learning so much newness. I still had to think too much, all the time, think about walking, every step, every almost missed step, every actual step. Was there a staircase or an elevator where I was going? Physical therapy conversations that I had with my therapist. I hear your voice repeatedly, Donna Twist, and I can't help this. I hated the reminders of my frail, weak gait, and your voice was familiar and soothing to my clumsy efforts, but it was constant and had to be with every step. "Lift, pick up your leg, raise up your leg, put it down right, careful, watch that raised concrete, and don't recurvatum (knee hyperextension, it hurts, and it is bad for your joint). Who knew that one-sixteenth of an inch could be dangerous—holy friggin' shit! (Unfortunately, I used the f-word, the real f-word, so many times now, I am stained with it verbally). This is a freaking nightmare, isn't it?

Okay, so by now you may be saying, "What happened to gratitude? Come on, it's not so bad—. Hey, girl, come on, you had this major spinal cord injury, you were totally paralyzed, and you walk! You study in a great college in New York City!! You live in an apartment in New York City!! (A dorm with three other, 'no-problem kids.)" "You still go out and meet guys," my friends would say, as if that was the premier of living, the essence.

Remember, I was twenty. Yes, it wasn't difficult to meet men. Keeping them around long enough was more challenging. After several relationships. That's generous; they were fun, but not relationships. When the guy I was dating would get to a specific point, when he was comfortable to ask me the relationship-killer question—*"So, is this it? Are you going to get any better?"*—I knew this relationship was over. "I've got to go—you don't understand." It's hard; even I don't like this body. How can I expect someone else to deal with me like this? Deal with me? I was crazed. Full of wants and emotions that moved so much deeper than the "no-problem" kids whose most puzzling question of the day would be about the shirt that they would be wearing tomorrow or dilemmas about their ski-trip plans.

It wasn't over for me as far as my constant struggles. I wasn't wearing those *blinders* on my eyes yet. I did look to my left or right, I did get distracted by people who were my age who were so carefree. I still would get thrown off course and still long for my old life, the easier one. I was still locked into those dreams beyond my neuro reality, dreams of this going away, and other dreams of being loved to any length, as in, until happily married after. I wasn't looking for marriage at this point, I wanted to date, and I was twenty, just like kids with no problems! Alone was no good. Alone was hard. Men were difficult. I couldn't compete with a "no problem" girl.

TAKE A PICTURE,
IT LASTS LONGER

Do you remember that phrase, when someone would stare, and we would say, "Take a picture, it lasts longer"? That was another chant of mine at the time: "The staring." I used to say this a lot, "I don't blend in, I get unnerved by all the staring at me." After the accident, when I was younger, I used to make up stories about the real story. When my friends and I would go out to bars, we would have to confirm which story I was using that night. It became comical and fun to see reactions on guys' faces. I had stories of skydiving and hitting a tree branch. My motorcycle story usually was a favorite because in that tale, I said that I was racing in an event and was bumped off the road, which made me fly 200 feet and I unfortunately landed on my head. That somehow seemed sexier than the real story. This story, my story, what "happened" to me, it was beyond people's' understanding. That was soooo frustrating. But why? Did I really expect them to "get it"? Get what? Understand that I was once like them without a thought for my next movement? Understand that I could literally be blown over by the wind? Think about that. The incapacity to move quickly enough, to react or move without a thought. And it did happen. On one excursion to begin a serious workout routine, I joined a club. I took a cab to the location, when I got out of the cab, the wind blew me over, down onto the street. People literally walked over me to get where they had to go. A kind man picked me up and snapped at the onlookers and others who passed me by. These were the people who didn't have a clue, they didn't get it. These were the able body people who without a thought, *lived so easily*. They could move freely without thinking, they could tie their shoelaces or button their blouse easily, but those actions would cause me all kinds of frustration. I did not wear blouses with buttons for years. Still don't. And I think it took me months to tie my shoes in whatever way I could. With so many other choices, why limit myself? Ha, I should have convinced myself of this years ago. There are so many choices we can make rather than obviously staying with the same thoughts and distractions.

BETTER THAN NORMAL

"Why do I give a shit if other people have problems?" I would say. "Laurie, you're becoming hard," my therapist said. "You're becoming indifferent, selfish." I didn't care. I used to compare situations, and mine usually triumphed. Nothing was shittier than what I was suffering. Nothing.

I was adjusting. I was back on obsessing about the *staring*, it became quite clear from my first outings post-rehab. It was a life unto itself, often dismissed and not popular to speak about, but I think part of my heart, mind and soul were torn there (in rehab) and then some. I sadly can say that I must have cried a million tears. The future for me was so dim. I was in this big time, and it felt like a prison sentence. In essence, it was, for I am a lifer, not funny, but true. Back in 1979, this type of injury was hardly known to many people. I had never heard of or met anyone who suffered a spinal cord injury. I got caught up again in the comparison game—that is, *the old me versus the new m*e or the *I used to be able to do this or that*, against the mighty reality that *No, you can do things now, it's just harder*. Or *yes, there are things you cannot do now* or *there are places you cannot go anymore*. It was the most awkward thing to juggle. Especially since I put myself into a culture and world (Fashion Institute of Technology) where staring at the latest beautified design on the most beautified people, faces and frames was—uh, what else? Normal!

Let's talk about NORMAL. You know that your life is not normal anymore when everything has been taken away. It is quick, that first realization of not-normal. Or it's the overwhelming need or desire to be back to your previous person, or lifestyle. Even if it wasn't so great, you'll take it. People say, "I just want everything to be the way it was. The way I knew it." Back to normal. It has a place; a feeling and it is desired. Even if your previous life was boring, mundane and average, when your *new* normal is "not as before." When all that is suddenly lost or there is permanent change, you realize how that previous version of you in whatever way, is ALL you want now. Oh, give me back my normal body, my normal life, my normal situation. Give me it back, it's my normal and it worked.

I had a difficult time switching on the old me and the new me. Sometimes I would forget I had this injury. Sounds odd, but in my head, I would think about doing something, or going somewhere as I always knew. The Laurie I knew before. I never knew if I should identify or relate or compare myself with disabled individuals or normal. Recently I was asking my friend. Who should I relate myself to? She answered quickly, "Laurie, your better than normal. You surpass normal, because you endure normal life normally, while being challenged. Therefore, you are better than normal!"

COPING SKILLS ARE EARNED

Mental stability was important here, and therapy reveals a lot. If you let it. I had told my psychotherapist at the time that Spider Man, yes, the character from the comic books, was climbing the tall building I saw outside her window. I was bored in therapy, I mean how many times can I say, "this sucks," and what is going to take that feeling away? Lying. The advice or coping mechanism: "Other people have difficulties, too." Or, "Try to see that you have been blessed, it could have been worse!" Really? That sounds good in conversation or as a theory, but my life events were showing me that it was time to stop, suck it up and look around. "Bend a little, Laurie, you're not the only one who has suffered." I hated this way of thinking. I would say to myself, "What do they know, those people who tell me these half-filled types of motivational phrases?" But again, every time, and I did start to notice, every single damn time I had a pity party, I would meet someone who would tell me stories of an illness of a child or themselves with a fatal sentence. Not that everyone died, but my situation was somehow "light" in comparison to theirs, and this happened a lot. Man, can't I *have* this? Can't I feel sorry for myself and enjoy it? Maybe I needed to hear this a lot. A lot because I was in self-pity often. It's a rough place to be, hurts so much, it's silent to others, but oh, so very loud inside my head. I can't shut it off at times. "Stop, I can't take this anymore, I can't!" I did feel for other people, I just didn't care at this point.

"You're going to be okay, people would say, you're doing well. You're in school, you're cute, you're smart, you are—you are, you are—" Come on, people. See, I'm disabled, don't you see this? I walk with a cane, a definite limp, my hand is all crooked and messed up and I can't run. I can't, can't, can't."

GOD HAS SOME SENSE OF HUMOR

"No, this is all I am probably going to be. If you mean, am I ever going to run? That kind of wellness?" That was my response to that "concerned for my future" boyfriend. I guess he felt that he could ask me this question. I somehow was waiting, this all felt too good to be true. I can do a lot, but there is a certain line I cannot cross over. I cannot say, "I am able-bodied," or "I am normal" again. I cannot do everything I used to do. This body is different in so many ways. The physical barriers were there, inside my body and outside my body. I had major limitations, no matter how good I looked standing still, and even that's questionable. I had postural issues, still do. Just one step, and it's clear, just one attempt to zip a zipper, you will see that line.

That boyfriend at the time had asked me that upsetting question. Truth was, he had met a girl runner when he used to jog in the mornings. It never bothered me that he went running. Well, it did. I had been running for four months before the accident. I knew the thrill and pains of the sport. Ironically, my current, and trendy, "running shoes" never had a "run" in them, they never got worn out like we did. I started to get very paranoid in the city. My current emotional state was feeding off that boyfriend rejection.

Back to my current focus. I needed to go on school outings for marketing classes that I was taking. Standing on the corner getting ready to cross the street was like asking someone to jump across the Grand Canyon. I couldn't do it. My legs were tight in a spasm, people were passing me by, and I was frozen. I was not happy. This was happening a lot now. On that corner, I silently prayed that my situation would change. *Oh God, please let my feet move—now!!*

"Nickel bag, dime bag, blow—Nickel bag, dime bag, blow." I heard this drug rap from a guy on the corner of Forty-Second Street and Eighth Avenue. It was his version of drug-dealing public relations, and he was standing a few feet away. I am frozen again, I cannot cross this street. The other side might as well have been Texas.

"Hey, sweetie pie, I noticed that five or six green lights have passed and you're still here. Need me to escort you across to the other side?" Maybe he thought I was a narc. I looked up at this guy, who just a few seconds before was selling drugs, and now he was my answer to prayer, my one and only rescue? I looked up to the sky, where God lives, "You have got to be kidding, God, you have a crazy sense of humor!" I screamed. "Here I am stuck on this corner asking for help, and this is who you send to help me?"

I looked around. No one else was offering to help me. No one else who seemed "okay" or someone who *looked* like a *good* person. I was desperate, and I took his arm and we walked to the other side. He bopped as he walked, and he spoke like the Sugar Bear cereal character. "Want me to walk you all the way home?" I replied, "No, that's okay, I got this now." I mean, come on, my being stretched as a human being was increasing. I was learning this new way of life. As he helped me and took my hand, I forced my face to have a smokescreen of "I don't care what I look like." My sanity needed this, this type of attitude. And I did. I walked the lie. I had to. It wasn't okay, but somehow it relaxed me when I got stuck again. I used to sing, "Can't get enough of that sugar crisp, sugar crisp, sugar crisp, it keeps me going strong!"

Again, on another outing for school, I needed a taxi, but now this is getting ridiculous! I felt the heat of that bright yellow monster's radiator on my leg, and then heard the siren of his horn as I shut down into statue mode. I was unable to move, frozen, as I stepped into the street to cross that afternoon.

I was visiting publishing houses for another class project, near Madison and Forty-Third Street. Trying to get to the perpetual "other side," I was in this "can't cross the street" season of transition again! The taxi driver was an inch away from my leg and honking his horn, as if I needed him to tell me that I am stuck here. "Yo, I cannot move and you're making it a thousand times worse." Then, "Hey, it's okay now, I got you!" Two handsome twins visiting New York for job interviews picked me up and placed me back on the curb. "What are you doing! Trying to get killed?" one of them screamed at me. Now a crowd was also screaming at the taxi driver and calling for the police! This was a scene, and I couldn't speak, but I wasn't going to go into the whole litany of my story, when the nice one with a warm touch hailed another cab, put me in it, kissed me, threw a $20 at the driver and said, "this better cover her fare." He shouted to me that they were from Chicago and going to back to JFK, and waved goodbye! I had genuine issues to deal with, both physical and emotional. These types of things started to happen more. Not the cute guy part, the panic.

I started to hate the lifestyle of New York because it is a "walking city." The best way to get around is walking and public transportation. This became harder, and somehow, I lost my love of the craziness, the rhythm that the city echoes. I couldn't get back in tune with that vibe, it scared me now and became too difficult. I didn't want to fight unnecessary battles now. I just wanted and needed a change for an easier lifestyle. After dozens of nights and days of crying, the paranoia got worse. I was miserable, feeling lousy. My days were ending at school, I had enough credits to graduate early, I stayed and took one of those groovy electives. I think it was perfume making.

REVLON, INC.

I was in my final year at FIT, it was my last year in college, and I had big decisions to make. What was I going to pursue in the job market? I was on track for internships that semester, so I was concentrating on that and making plans with roommates to share an apartment when we finally did graduate. All typical issues of current seniors, but anything typical for me. I had such anxiety about everything, it all seemed so mountaintop to me and unattainable in my mind. Or did it? I was doing wonderful things at that point, some that I never imagined while lying in that hospital bed just a brief time ago.

Revlon Inc. sent a message to my HR coordinator at school, and she told me to go to their corporate offices on Fifth Avenue and Fifty-Ninth, the General Motors building. It was February, cold, and on this fine morning of a terrific opportunity, it was pouring rain. "Taxi!" Well, the cab stopped a little ahead of me, about six feet too far, and a guy ran and hijacked it! Son of a b@*^h! But it turned out for good. My taxi, the one I actually got in, had an angel named José Garcia. (I got used to looking at the driver's name tags when I got into taxis, so, God forbid, I could remember them if anything bad happened. (Advice from a concerned mother, let's just put it that way!)

On the trip uptown, José broke the ice and asked me why I had the cane. I crankily told him my story in the short version because I was concentrating on the interview and really had no time to chat with a cab driver! I hurried through my "story" because I was going over the interview tips from my counselor. I heard crying, and I looked up. Sure enough, he started to cry! I noticed he had tissues and was wiping his eyes, and he showed me a picture of his daughter, same age as me, and then he asked me where the hell was I was going in such rotten weather! "A Revlon interview," I yelled through the window. "I'm so excited but scared, this is a great chance to work in the forecasting department."

"Uh, what is that? I know they do makeup." "Yes, well, forecasters work with all facets of the colors that will be in future

95

seasons for not only makeup, but also in fashion, home goods, and even autos." Geez, I sounded so "interview ready." Anyway, it's pouring rain, and we pull up to the GM building and the outside entrance has about forty-five steps to the entrance in the shape of a pyramid. "Oh, shit look at all those steps, how the hell you going to get up there? I'm going to lose my medallion for this!" As he said that, José put his car flashers on, double-parked on Fifty-Ninth Street and practically carried me up on his hip, all those steps, and got me to the front door, kissed me and said, "You better get this f'n job now!" Dear José, I did!

Two weeks—that's all the job lasted! Revlon announced a few days into my hire that they were having a financial restructuring, and that all employees hired in the previous sixty days were terminated. Ugh.

Are you serious? I got the dream job and now it's gone, serious therapy for this one! This was not good, their financial restructuring, meant back to the job hunt. Sorry, José, we did our best.

I got a new job at a top advertising agency, Ted Bates Inc. The account my group worked on was snack foods and tooth paste. I always laughed at that; eat junk, and then keep away the cavities. It was boring. This was pre-computer error and watching demographics meant scanning books of data, only these books had hundreds of pages and there were many. I wasn't liking this counting of eyeballs and it seemed that the group ate candy all day while making efforts to improve their clients market share. A few interviews later and a new job, I lived my own small version of "The Devil Wears Prada." She wasn't a Miranda Priestly, but I was a personal assistant to a woman and her partner, a rag man. That is a nickname, a not-so-kind term, for men (mostly) who bought and sold textiles. This company did knockoffs, copies of runway couture, with the slightest change here and there. It was legit, and the practice was accepted. But with the annoying sexual overtone remarks from the Rag, and after a few months of typing my boss's younger brother's request for his third rehab visit, I really thought—this is not what I want to be doing. I hated the city now, I had to leave, I could not get around. I need a car, I need a different lifestyle. Goodbye, Miranda, and so long, Rag.

My physical tasks of everyday life were becoming demanding and challenging. I was getting dissatisfied with the silliness of my career choice. Not that there's anything wrong with that world, it's just that I felt that I was not able to compete. The workplace and people or the culture at that time were not different-friendly or disabled-friendly as things seem to be now.

Some of my professors at school did not care or treat me any different than anyone else. But I did need a measure of grace. In my Industrial Knitting class, our tasks were to operate a 30ft. long machine, the same used in a textile factory. I am not sure if you've ever been near one of these gigantic and powerful machines. They are impressive for knitting purposes, but not so user friendly. We had to produce a sample knit piece and more importantly thread it. This worth was significant only to the prof. I went often to the lab because I was afraid to literally hold the spool of wool and carefully feed the thread into this monster.

Being careful was an understatement, "it could take a finger or two," the lab techs favorite expression. Well, I could not do it, my fingers and hands shut down into spasms with even the thought of it. Long story short, my class grade was compromised, according to the prof and I was stuck with his crappy attitude and a 2x2 inch sample of my work. It was totally unfair, that he put so much weight of my grade on whether or not I could physically do this task.

In my media class, that prof thought it would be *fun* to draw 28 blank lines across the chalk boards. "Run up and put your name in the spot you want for your final project." Guess who got #28. Last, as in *I CAN'T RUN MORON*. I got an A+, my classmates voted my final TV commercial #1.

I currently love seeing people in wheelchairs *rolling* the catwalk for brave fashion designers. My roommate, a fashion design major, would have loved this. She measured her final to my frame, size 6 , same as her mannequin. Unfortunately, I could not *walk* (runway) for her. Her final project which was white legging ski pants and a suede fringe jacket were ready for the slopes but not with me in them. Her model for this came down with the flu and her replacement wasn't exactly the figure for this outfit. I cried when she asked the dean to let me do it, but… Back then, if you did not walk out of *Vogue's* current "season" page, which covered you from hair, makeup and, of course, latest style trends, you did not measure up, and the feeling was, " do not even bother," and this was for everyone, not just me, that girl with the cane. The fashion world loves to use images of uniqueness, they encourage the individual flare. That's all cool, but they never carried it over into people that are truly exceptional. Just because people roll instead of walk; or walk with a device or whichever way they can move, their different is worthy. They want to love what they look like and have their own style. Inclusion comes in many shapes and forms.

Since I walked with a cane, most people did not know how to handle me. I still did not, either, and I recently complained that to a good friend that "back then I was so lost, I did not know who I was and how to adjust. I always hoped people would understand me, but they rarely did." "Laurie," she replied, "you always made it look so easy, easy that you were well-adjusted and despite the physical struggle, you had yourself all together in so many ways. Your hair always looked great, your clothes, and you were so motivated; you even went to college for crying out loud! Lots of people who didn't go through what you went through don't even go to college! Your story is one of triumph! It was tragic, but you made it triumphal! You made things happen for yourself! You came back, when honestly, we did not think you would be able to handle the limitations. Especially you. Ever since grammar school, I always remember you doing all kinds of sports. In school, we both played volleyball, softball, paddleball, and I remember you were a runner. We thought you were going to go crazy just for that alone."

I was blown away. "I hid it that well? You mean you all thought I was this brave little trooper, and that I had a great attitude?" Well, I did wear a mask, I guess, because that was the farthest person from whom I really was. I was a lengthy list of opposites, a learning curve, only I was the curve. If being normal was the curve, there was a tennis match in my head, and I never knew where I was in this. I kept going above the curve, because I was getting stronger or thought I could "beat" this. It was the idea of going back to normal or even being better than my current normal; that often kept me going. Or I felt like I was way below the curve, way below it. The skill set to learning this would require living *it* every second of the day. A skill set to learn how to handle my limitations was the key. How do I react to myself? I need to remember to settle myself because the smallest frustration would push my buttons. When I could not open the jar of peanut butter, it was a challenge. Managing walking around people in a crowd, as in the school elevators. What if it rocks or jerks, will I fall?

Will I look like an idiot? Sorry, but it goes through your head. Sometimes it felt like a scene we have already seen in a movie. Someone in a first person shot, is walking down a crowded NYC street with headphones on. The music is loud and the other people on the left and right are fast forward moving all around. Everyone is moving quickly but you're in a tunnel of your own motion. The movement is all too fast to catch up to. I felt like that a lot when I first started walking around the city. I did use and carry my Walkman, it helped me keep my own beat amongst the airstream of others. I was still an extensive list of newness and adjusting; this would describe me best. The list was open-ended or labeled "uncharted territory." Sometimes, I did not know who I was; I was Laurie who had an SCI, who was told she would never walk again, hurt, readjusting, and recovering. The other me was, look at me now, I am walking, proud and looking forward? Such a conflict. Again, I had to find a balance, do I sit and cry all day, or do I do what I got to do, even if it's slower and different now?

The summer-in program was the place to be for a few years. I took 6 credits for 6 weeks, which were quick and easy. I had one class in the afternoon twice a week and one evening three times a week or vice a versa. So, then the rest of the day or night was mine.

I met Jack at a FIT street fair. He was selling earrings and had quite the smile. He was a cuter version of a famous drummer; according to Jack, he told everyone he was. Jack lied about it so often he loved it. It was hysterical, he sounded just like him, dressed like him and convinced people he was Phil Collins. I thought he was crazy, but we had the best summer in New York City. He taught me something. Sometimes it is easier to pretend. You can pretend or develop another image of yourself when you *need* to. You can put on your tough girl face, or the type that says, "here I am, it is me. If you don't like it, don't look. If it is easier to put on the happy face at times, put it on and smile large. If you don't know what to do or think or how to be, then make believe." A unique approach to my situation I thought, but it worked. He said, "you do it already. You tell people the motorbike story or parachute jump. That's pretending." I guess I did. And he said, "when we are selling jewelry and meeting people, they don't see the "handicapped" version of you. They see someone amazing."

It helped me come out of myself, the scared self. The one I've been speaking about, with all those inner overthinking stupid lies.

We were just *friends* and Jack hated that. I went with him to all the local street festivals and flea markets, selling jewelry. On one particular night, a customer stopped me and said, "Laurie P? Is that you? Look at you, I cannot believe how good you look! It was Mary, a nurse from Rusk. I knew her well. We hugged, and I cried. She reminded me of all the stupid things they did to me for laughs. Her and Susan, another RN, in the slower hours or when they felt like a good laugh would dress me as if I was going out. With shoes and coat, they would close me up in the electric bed like a sandwich. I guess after that long of a stay, and the craziness of it all, I didn't mind their escapades for me. Mary stopped for that moment to say to me, "wow, your living in the city, your standing tall and walking strong, and going to college. A far cry from the girl who cried a lot and thought nothing good would ever happen to her again." She told me that she remembered she was on vacation when I took my first steps. When she came back on the floor, she saw me walking for the first time. I was initially using the wheelchair as a walker, and she had to go in the bathroom to cry. Her and Susan, were two of the nurses whom I came to know and lean on in so many ways. The funny thing was that they weren't that much older than me. But they were nurses and had all authority. We hugged again goodbye, it was a great confidence boost to realize again from whence I came...at least I have some fond memories of those days, and some of the nurses were my cheerleaders, they got to see a happy ending story, amidst all that pain.

Jack was right. I got the confidence to pretend and make believe again. I got a new face, I got back some *tude*.

RAW HONESTY: DOES EVERYTHING HAVE TO BE SO HARD?

Reality was screaming again. I was at an end-of-the-year party in my dorm apartments, and I was excited to even be invited because this was the "coolest" guy on campus, and he personally knocked on my door to ask me. At the party, amid all this grooviness, I had to use the bathroom, and quickly. Of all the times to have to go—OH, God, not now! But yes, I couldn't even get down the hall to my apartment. This embarrassment was forever, it seemed. I had to live with this, live with issues that were too uncomfortable to speak about; heck, most people can't even say the word "fart" publicly. Man, spinal cord injury people live with this and, yes it stinks!! I spent what seemed to be the next hour in his bathroom, and he kept knocking and asking me if I was okay. OKAY?? I'm going to need therapy for this.

Again, what is a shrink going to say? I gave up on them, I thought they were all full of s*%t, also. I mean what magic words were they going to say that would make me feel better? What epiphany was I going to come to realize peace? I wanted it all to go away, to stop. To be over, and to wake up as if this never happened. — Well, it did. Get over it and roll with the punches. Hmmm, I wonder where that phrase came from, but it is true. Sometimes when there is no answer, or life gets so difficult, you have to roll with the punches or the bullshit that life has thrown your way. Pity parties, or some say self-hate, some might *add* these to the *lengthy list* of tantrums and drama that we, who are struggling through an illness or life-altering issue go through, we who have endured the pain of an event or major loss, we who hate to be labeled as *different*.

"But really, Laurie, there is always *someone to talk to*," as in psychotherapist. It's just that I did not "buy" the therapy thing anymore. That was the usual direction I was entertaining when I felt like the *circus* was back in town. Or when I felt *different*. I knew that it was good to speak to someone. Maybe I did not want to admit that. This wasn't easy, and I am glad that I projected an "all together" image, but really, I just tried to live like it never happened. Whether this is delusional or denial or just fierce attitude because I realized *ain't* nobody going to do for you but you. I think that's a song, or it should be! There was a back and forth of *I can't* and or *I can* do this, every single day.

I could not talk again and again about all my feelings. I tried and submitted to all the techniques in therapy, but they did not seem to work for me. I am immune to mental therapy! I can appreciate the good thoughts and positive thinking and good gratitude "TUDE" — but as soon as I take a step or as soon as a body part doesn't work, that all disappears. I am right back "there" — and it seems senseless to me to think a good thought and then it only lasts for seconds. I was in this tennis match for life. I learned that these times of back and forth, sorrow and regret often become your frenemies. They keep you in a small box, a sneaky box that opens and then the lid shuts fiercely on your fingers. It stings, but you go back for more. You love to hold onto the hurt, it is safe, you know it like the back of your hand. You're isolated in your own world and thoughts. It is what you learned to use as a defense mechanism. OH, my therapist would be proud because I used that term! A defense mechanism to justify my anger, and all it did was make me angrier. But you hate them, an enemy's best secret is disguising itself as a close friend. Don't let them!

Back adjusting to a new routine at home and working, I still wanted to be doing fun things in the city, I still had friends there. Back then, Brooklyn was a big negative. It was too far, and it was NOT Manhattan. Things have certainly changed because the house I grew up in is now worth one million freaking dollars! That became frustrating as well, since I could not use buses or trains, and I had to rely on the Medicare bus or some other transportation, *arranged*, by my vocational counselor! Um, not exactly groovy. I wanted desperately again to escape the "handicapped" section. This issue of "getting around" was huge. My walking dilemmas about getting paranoid and *frozen* on street corners were still active. These issues kept me grounded, kept me angry.

I MET A GUY

This was the 80s, a time where, in the romance world, you met a guy, dated and then married, unlike now, when it seems that marriage is on a downturn, but that was the norm of the time. Paul would come to visit in the city and we would go explore SOHO, East Village and other new groovy neighborhoods and good eats. I had just decided after the last burned-up relationship, that with the next guy I met—no sex (going to go real slow)?? Upfront, that's how it is, sorry, trying new things this time. Paul didn't flinch, he went right along, maybe he thought I would cave. It helped that he was a Christian guy. I didn't exactly know what that meant because all guys said a lot of things, but he really lived what he preached.

Who was this guy? I felt safe and didn't worry about the usual drama, there wasn't any, Paul was easy. We dated on and off because of school. I was too close to finishing. I think I had one more semester until I would graduate. I had many mixed feelings about our relationship. There was also a third person involved, and that person was the relationship that Paul had with God. I should not have been surprised by this because I had met Paul at a barbeque. I was set up by my mom and her new church friend, and we played softball. He included me, I hit the ball, and someone ran for me. I liked that about him, and he is still that way, he's an encourager, he loves to be involved with people, including difficult people. Not me, I was tired of difficulty, and I was willing to do anything to be far away from it. My newest difficulty was that I was not the only affection that Paul had, and I had to share him with God? Wow, I did not know that people had that type of deep and real relationship with the higher power, the man upstairs, God, the big guy up in heaven. I couldn't understand his love of God. I felt like I was the outsider looking in, and I do not think Paul knew or understood my intimate feelings. I was young and so needy of a solid friendship, one-on-one, not three's a crowd. In spite of this, Paul became my best friend, this was new to me, he was male. He was different, and this difference was good for me. It was a critical time for me. Previously, I had dated a *separated* man, unknowingly, of course, and then dated the dream guy who ran off with a "runner."

I knew that Paul was a keeper, that guy you bring home. He was sincere, and he liked me in spite of how I walked, and how insecure I felt, and he always made me feel special and safe. I had to adjust to all this niceness and honesty. It was the way he treated me that made him hard to ignore. He's attentive, and thoughtful of my needs; he learned quickly that he had to be mindful of intricate things about me that most people overlooked. Always opening the door, knowing that I could trip on trivial things, holding my hand, and being my support in so many ways. He was cute, tall and strong, with a smile that melted my fears. Our relationship strengthened during our times apart. I loved his voice over the phone. He would call me before going to sleep and he kept me focused.

Paul was active in his faith. He had a one-on-one relationship where he knew that he could open God's word in the Bible and find peace, joy, hope and a direction for his future. He was solid in his faith because he trusted in the pureness of the scriptures. Me? I opened the Bible and had no clue of what I was going to find…. but I did have a start! Back in the hospital, the pastor, Reverend Mercaldo, gave me a New Testament and that note. He wrote to me and said, "Begin in the first book of this New Testament, the book of John. *This is a new life map for you to follow, trust Him and He will help you on your road,"* he wrote. Wow, I treasured that note from someone who followed God's direction (Reverend Mercaldo was told to visit me in his dreams), and I love that he extended himself in faith to touch my hands and pray! I am so glad for honest faith. He brought me to a place of hope and faith in God, whom I honestly did not know at this time. I went to his funeral over a year later. When I walked into the funeral parlor, his sweet wife greeted me. She actually knew who I was. She said, "you must be Laurie!

My husband prayed and spoke about you every day. I was amazed and thankful.

With few exceptions, most people I have shared this with will always point me to the fact that God is a huge part of this story: "He wants you to realize just how much He loves you. Laurie, He saved you in the pool, you did not die, you went through a tragedy, but you came out okay! Why are you so hurting?" Hurting? Is there an expiration date to this all, am I supposed to "get better" already? Is everyone thinking that I should be okay "by now" and I should be able to accept this and move on? Acceptance without resignation! That was the message from a new counselor I was seeing. "Laurie, you must accept what happened and move forward, do not resign and quit." Really? If there was one message I needed to hear, that *moving on* message was not the one. I was living this. Moving forward? I thought I was doing that!

Is it just in my head and *my own, bad thinking private conversations*? If we are honest, you may be wishing, as I do, to secretly write an email like, "DEAR GOD, does everything have to be so hard? I mean, my struggles are major, and I know there are so many other people hurting, enduring and living in constant struggling. Does it have to be this way?" Somehow, some way can you hear me?

I would often try to remember to seek God, and I felt like I hadn't given Him enough of my heart, because I was still angry. I am a mess. Now I'm trying to believe and have faith, but I'm failing, the hugeness of it is too much sometimes and I am angry, I am ungrateful, I am tired of hope, I am tired of praying. I want to be that great witness but can't, I want to get the second part of my miracle, but I doubt. Something in me is ruining the plans. I feel like the Israelites wandering for forty years. So close to the promised land, but will I have the necessary epiphany or ingredient for a second miracle? Will it be too late, did I waste my life? Is my complaining about this hard and new difficult life keeping me just outside of the miracle?

KNOCK, KNOCK

As I said before, I heard that knock, when in the exact moment of drowning or death, I did hear God tell me, "If you do not come up, you will not come back." What do I do with this story—is this just for me?

I opened that door a long time ago. I was desperate. Somehow, I managed to *top* one difficult life changing painful event for another.

I thought I was smarter than this. I thought I was smarter than *it*. The recurring pain in the butt, haunting and crappy memory. *It* just wins too often. But I have managed, through tear and effort, to conquer most challenges. I have learned to recognize the junk that is coming to ruin my day and shove it back down; move it into the bad files folder, it threatens my security.

I do this still. If I think about it, I currently do mental war games in my head about how I can win over my own negative vibes and have a productive day. I do make an effort. I pray as I stretch and talk to myself, and I talk to God. I'm alone, so it sometimes gets scary, but this is now called "self-talk," it's now called a good thing.

I needed my life to make some sort of sense. All the "why" questions; the "why" circus. That's what I call it, it's a place where we get stuck, isn't it? A place in your head that's on all the time, and even the default button has no other option. It's on auto loop and you cannot "unloop" it. The tapes, as some people call it. We ask, "Why? Why did this happen, why did I have to do such and such? Why, again, why did this happen? When there is no cure, no surgery, no exercise routine, no medication, countless hours of telling a mind therapists (psychiatrists)— "This sucks," I put my hand on the doorknob and opened that door. I made the effort.

Why not? I trekked and tried through some of the other alternate "seeking" expeditions of faith, meditation or even sometimes a useful bout of denial and mind-over-matter techniques. Roads that address the question, "Does this life have a meaning?" These are the thoughts you contemplate while lying in a bed for countless hours, days, weeks, months, and years. These are the thoughts you ask when you know that you died and that you were given that second chance and wonder why you're still here.

I stepped out in faith, as they say, I brought all the garbage, that stuff and the scenes my brain was entertaining. We are encouraged to bring this pain, bring that circus to the cross. It is there, that all "this" is to be dealt with and free you. Because God's gift of redemption, grace and mercy begins and ends there. It's tricky, it's a matter of humbleness and a washing of our pride.

I did not know how to deal with my anger. How else could I explain, it seemed for me, that there is validity and a justification in being mad and angry. I am still angry sometimes, and I also needed to forgive God? Yes, I said that, I mean in *my* hurt and confusion I doubted whether all this really happened as I stated. Oh goodness, I could hear a lot of noise coming from that statement. Or did I hit my head so hard that I am delusional and grasping for anything that sounds good? It isn't that we *forgive* God, that's not possible. It is a *seeing* and a letting go, *seeing* God as my rescuer, my redeemer and giving me another chance to live.

Can I escape my pride, and my anger? Am I able to be humble enough or grateful enough to have the faith to say, "God, I trust you. You saved me from death literally and lifted me back to life. I should be the happiest person alive, shouldn't I?"

It's in those conversations that we wish that we could get the answer, the *it's okay, this make sense now* answer. The kind that when you're talking, and He listens. Even though, I wish He would answer in a more current fashion of direct, quick and convenient text messages! But He did send those answers! I wasn't ready to understand yet. I opened and briefly read those messages and had forgotten to go back and absorb His provision and love, and it is me who needs to turn from my own self and my garbage and take His lead with a new beginning. Time to move on, time to forgive yourself. Gratitude is thankfulness, gratefulness, appreciating, recognizing and acknowledgment.

It all seems so simple in an effortless way, and it should be natural, shouldn't it? I maintain that for me it is effort. The process of turning off your nightmare thoughts, the ones that harm, and then to work at seeing the positive in this mess and keeping hopeful, is the better way to be, this is a healthier attitude. But I struggle, I sometimes can't. It is a daily battle. The battle or tennis match that I have referred to, or my going back and forth, usually is my enemy, and that is myself. I cannot escape this, the very thing that I wish I could. I wish that I could go back in time, a time machine sounds like a great ride right now.

"Why, Laurie? With what you've been through, you really are blessed, in that you do walk and are not in a wheelchair. You have a wonderful husband, he really is, and a beautiful son who is doing so well. You need to see it in this light."

A friend just said, "I can't believe how much you are hurting, still." It is like this, no even keel here. This hurts, there are seasons of abundance and seasons of want. Lord, we pray for rain! I try to feel happy and joy and feel okay with my situation, but I have lost so much. I guess I am feeling *half-empty glassed* right now. I am in a glass globe with its whirling white papers, like confetti pieces all tagged with my painful events, swirling around me. I look at the titles and cry, there are a lot of them—writing this book has shaken my globe and the confetti is flying. Yuk! the very places I don't want to go, I go. (The very things I don't want to do, I do, and the very things I want to do, I do not).

I do tell myself, "Come on Laurie, get with it. Trust in the good things that have risen from this. You should be hopeful now. You have been spared and given so much, a lot of grace came your way. You have been married thirty years to a man who loves you, sometimes I think more than himself. He does, it's unreal how much he has given you and still wants to."

LEAVE AND CLEAVE

I was desiring and considering moving to a simpler lifestyle. The easy living of a one-story ranch house with a pool in the backyard appealed to me; unfortunately, it was in south Florida. Paul would have to leave his job, family, friends and Sam, his thirteen-year-old black Lab! This was a turning point in our relationship since it was unexplored territory. I was used to things changing a lot and adapting to it, but Paul had a rough transition. We met our friend Alice for lunch one day, by her usual mysterious invite. She had a way of knowing what was going on in our lives and was a dear woman of deep spiritual insight. She had a present for us, an oil painting of an angel. On the back of it she wrote: "God told Abraham: 'Leave your country, your family, and your father's home for a land that I will show you. I will bless you there." It was so God-appointed. This gave us the assurance that we could leave and go from our safe surroundings and transition there. We got married and moved. It was kind of sad because we were leaving our family and friends, but so exciting for us! Did I ever mention that I usually go, or things happen in my life that go from zero to one hundred? We settled in that one-story ranch home with a pool, and it was awesome.

We had no clue what anything costs to set up a house. When we moved we really had only wedding presents, clothes and my piano. We had to buy furniture, bedding, everything, but it was fun. It was time to break out the wedding presents, especially the pots and pans. That meant cooking! In my mother's house, the kitchen was her domain. She loved it and ruled it. When I was younger, she used to say, "Watch me do this or that, that's how I learned." And so, I did. It came natural to me, cooking was soothing. Except when my fingers couldn't open packages; those were my challenges. For my first dinner party, I cooked for my Aunt Tina and Uncle Joe, who lived nearby. She is my mother's older sister and a great cook at that. I committed to the invite, although I panicked afterwards. You see, I come from a family, an Italian American family that rates the dinner! They give a score from zero to ten. The sauce, or gravy, the meatballs, the macaroni, (we never called it pasta) everything! To my surprise, Aunt T gave my meatballs a very high score of 8.5! This quad can cook!

THE POSITIVE SIGN +

A baby! I remember seeing the positive sign on the cube, on the pharmacy pregnancy test kit, which I still have! It was a cold winter when we traveled to New York City to visit for Christmas that year. I was feeling a little run down because I had spent the last few days shopping like a crazy person in the malls in Florida. I have to admit, I still am amazed at how much I did when I was younger. I walked the entire mall, shopped and carried the bags back to my car! That year, it was a cold twenty-nine degrees in south Florida, and that meant it would be so much colder up in New York, where it was zero when we landed at LaGuardia. Some hours later, we arrived at my brother's house after midnight. I slept for the next thirty hours before my sister-in-law suggested that I may be Prego! No, not now, I wasn't prepared to be a mommy. I was still learning about me. I was married only two years, I needed more time! Honestly, I didn't even know if quadriplegics have babies. I wasn't sure if it was possible. I doubted that I was pregnant until that second line, that line in the test, which crossed over the first line, confirmed it. I am pregnant! I remember being in the upstairs bathroom and looking into the mirror. I said to myself, "This is forever, how are you going to do this?" The cheering from downstairs made this one of the happiest days of my life. My husband's face and tears answered that question. "*We* are going to do this!"

You should have seen me pregnant. Ha, I carried us (me and baby), through all nine months. Actually, at seven months, the doctor suggested bed rest. When the day came, it was early morning and I woke up to a wet bed. You can prepare all you want, as we did, but it still was a comical event as usual. At six a.m., my water breaks, I call to my husband, who is shaving! He gets crazy with joyful hysteria and runs out of the house with half his face full of lather, only to remember that he needed to bring *us* to the hospital.

Because the anesthesiologist did not want to give me an epidural. The plan was that I would be given Demurral. Only 25 mg? I said, "that ain't gonna be enough." They gave me an additional 50. After two hours with only one minor contraction, concerned faces told me that something wasn't right. "Mrs. Z how are your contractions?" When I did not respond in a normal face full of pain and discomfort, the nurse ran out, and she came back with two doctors and some machines. They put a monitor onto the baby's skull, and the doctored ordered the "pit." That was Pitocin to bring on the contractions, which it did. Later that afternoon, I woke up to the doctor yelling for me to push, and a nurse was on top of me. She was in my bed pushing her elbows down on my belly to help move the baby down the birth canal. I was foggy from the drugs, exhausted, and he wants me to "push like a bowel movement." Yeah right, he doesn't realize, that didn't happen often on its own, so his coaching is annoying me now. With God's grace, and fifteen minutes to spare before they went C-section, I did manage to push, and our son Jordan was born! He weighed eight pounds and was twenty-one inches long, healthy and screaming, and it was a beautiful healthy scream! This quad had a baby!

Bringing the baby home to a house full of family and friends was terrifying to me. I now had to be a mommy, I was physically tuned out and not exactly sure I could handle the demands. Since I wasn't breastfeeding, I was anxious to do the bottle routine and get him fed. The first night home I was sitting in my kitchen with half a dozen of people coming to see him for the first time. I had the plastic liners and his formula ready; but I struggled big time with stretching those darn plastic bags tight over the bottle and then screw the nipple on top. I lost focus and spilled it all over and cried. How am I going to do this?

I did it, I ripped a few bags in the effort but it worked out. I had to learn how to be extremely patient from now on, I had my own struggles and now new little struggles and I didn't want the baby to hear me when I ranted on how difficult this was.

Jordan was such a good little boy. This was more grace my way! I had such a connection to him that I cherished, and this made Paul wonder at times. I had that baby-mommy thing, knowing every little grunt and coo he made, even if he was in his crib. Another miracle was lying in the room next door. This baby kept me alive, as much as he needed me to survive. The physical challenge of holding him became one of the hardest things for me. I didn't want someone else to do this. I did all the long cranky nights and rocked him to sleep, but this meant

I also got the privilege and gift of nursery rhymes and singing him back into la la land! What a gift. I used to sing him to sleep, thanking God because it wasn't that long ago when I was told, "You will not be the same." They really meant, "We're not sure if you should have babies. The pregnancy may weaken you too much." Well, it did weaken me, but worth every stretch mark and lose abdominal muscle. As he grew, he was getting bigger and heavier and I did drop him at seven months on the tile floor! What kind of mommy was I going to be? How can I possibly take care of him when I and myself were enough for a day? We put him in a baby stroller, deemed only for the house. It was small and perfect to hold him for me, so I could move from room to room and not worry about carrying him or dropping him again. Oh, the guilt of a new mother.

I must have impressed my girlfriend who had her baby later in life. One morning I pick up the phone, and I hear, "How the hell did you do this!" I heard her baby crying in the background, and she was overwhelmed. I laughed and enjoyed the moment. I was proud of my efforts and ability to care full time for Jordan, although I could not have done it without the help from Paul and more importantly my mother! She moved down to Florida to be near us and she helped me tremendously. I also think that since Jordan was born on her birthday, she had new tears, tears of joy; she got a beauty from all those ashes.

"YOU HAD A CANE, I HAD A POCKETBOOK"

I did it! On my own I took Jordan to the pediatrician for all his appointments, took him to gym and tumble classes, art classes, park play dates, etc. Three-year-old pre-school, four-year-old—all his little school outings. I did. I am amazed at this gift. These were good days and nights. Children do this to our lives. We become young again and have fun with them. They live for a small time in a separate reality, and it's kind and sweet and hopeful!

It was hard to be depressed around his bright eyes, curly hair and cutie pie face. I was too busy and exhausted half the day. My limitations and poor self-image carried over to my mothering abilities. I had my own way of doing things, and now I felt measured up again to now a new norm of people, the Mommies crowd. I wondered if they would accept me and Jordan because I was "that mom, the one with the cane," or some other phrase that labeled me as "handicapped," only no one ever wanted to say that—at least not to your face. You don't only hear the whispers, you feel them too.

I felt isolated sometimes, and I always had the feeling that it was me overthinking. It was difficult being this new mom, and now I feared that these negative vibes spilled over onto my baby's life. Will he feel isolated as well? I just wanted to *be a part of*, I would think, *it's still me here, still me but inside a different body*…kind of mantra. These new people I am around, they just don't know. They don't know me as I was, or how far I have come. My body looks like it did, once. I did manage a close *normal* sometimes, only there are major differences and I don't mean cellulite. I am sure, but this may get a chuckle out of the people who know what I am referring to. When you're amongst able-bodied women, those women don't have a clue. When they just complain away about *their damn cellulite* that they have, because now their sorrowful lives are somehow compromised. They are saddened because they don't look the way they used to, and

117

they can't wear those cute little shorts like they used to. When you're trying to walk again—stand up straight, now lift your legs, clear the ground, push, engage the core, and repeat this in the other leg, simultaneously—only to realize that you took only a few steps, across the room, which seemed like a hard-ass workout, you think, "Girl, I'll take that cellulite, I'll take it and rub it everywhere on my body if it meant I could walk or run!"

I promised a long time ago that I would *not* let my depression be an overpowering, neon-blinking sign above my head. I vowed to hide being so damn scared all the time. I also vowed that I would be a little crazy and do fun stuff even though it took every ounce of energy I could get out of this body. Sometimes, my life is a workout! You need to understand what my body was dealing with. Even three years later, my body felt weakened by the pregnancy. We all know how our bodies change after children, and my body was definitely compromised. But I did it! This quad had a baby! I used to say that a lot. I never thought it would happen, I thought I was *okay* if I didn't have any children, but this was special, he was a special gift. Jordan was my champion. Later, I had three other pregnancies, but they all miscarried.

I got over the fear of those mommy gangs, and we went solo for a while, we made our own fun. We did lots of reading and creating, we did a lot of action-hero fun, too. Aisle 5A in Toys R Us, was our usual hang out. As early as age two, we used to walk together holding hands and we would always tap each other with our thumbs I think the tapping kept us in time with each other. It was amazing, my little son understood I was a beat or two or three, slower than everyone else.

Jordan was ready to go to preschool at age 3 at a little Christian Academy nearby. We worried that he would have a lot of separation issues because he was an only child. Well, so much for him crying, because I was the one who needed hugs and tissues. I peeked through the classrooms door window, and he met a friend. I kept waiting for him to notice, but I guess his new little playmate Josh, kept him amused for the morning. I met a friend also. A transplanted New Yorker like me, we noticed each other right away. We connected immediately and spent the next few months on the beach reminiscing about our hometown. Later on, she told me, *I liked you right away. I saw you and your son and thought, wow she is amazing, even with her difficulties. Laurie, I saw no difference, you had a cane, I had a pocketbook.* You have to love the vibe. New Yorkers are one of a kind.

Out with my morning coffee pals, I read in the local paper that a golf pro would be giving lessons for *Physically Challenged* people and he proudly pictured his star player, a 12-year-old boy, with a leg amputee. I liked the new term for people like me. Physically Challenged. To me this term, says, *I am challenged, not discontinued.* I thought wow, I would love to try this. So, I dropped off Jordan early and went to meet Frank the golf instructor. He said, "I like to be on the greens early to escape the heat." I agreed, and thought, *ahh, it is refreshing and cool, and no Barney.* I'd like to escape that. I had enough of that big purple dude singing songs and dancing with a tambourine.

Frank set me up on the driving range with clubs and a bucket and waited. I was getting myself ready to hit the ball following his instructions. This endeavor sure fit me to the "t," a line my friend used to say. *Laurie, you are either crazy or one of the more strongest persons I know. You do more things than most people, and they don't have challenges like you.* It was again a time when I forgot that I had a disability. I never thought of myself *as.* It's weird. But that's what people were always amazed at. I was just being me. I missed being active or doing sports. So, I attempted them just as I am.

In golf, I forgot that when you wind up to hit the ball your body is torqued and your off balance for a sec before you finish the swing. Well, I swung and missed the ball completely, but I was able to recover. I stepped quickly to even out my stance and used the club to lean on. The laws of physics were definitely against me here. My swing was unconventional, but it worked. I missed the first, missed the second, but hit the third ball 150 yards! This quad can golf!

Frank was surprised. He said, if you could do that again, you can do a circuit. He was excited and started to figure a plan of golf workouts for me to prepare. He was serious! Unfortunately, that was the end of my golf career, a few nights later, while playing with Jordan I couldn't move. I injured my L-4 and rehabbed for six months.

It was rough, but we got through it, I changed my sport activities. I went back to the pool and swimming, this was safer.

Jordan was great, and he had many friends, which always confused my neighbors. We always had kids over to the house. They thought I had a lot of children. I took him to every dang baseball, basketball and football practice and game. We loved it, and we made wonderful friends from his school and our church. Through Jordan, we made friendships that we will forever cherish. His classmates and their parents became part of our family. I will always be grateful for that extended family that nurtured him and helped mold him. I'm remembering through his life all the things I've accomplished. I gave life and that life gave me back a life. I am amazed, the list is long, it's special. I feel better to remember and grateful I've had the chance to love and be loved by my flesh, my own littleness—and now he's all grown-up. I am thankful that he has a wonderful job and is being groomed for a bright future and just moved to an apartment. A great son. Ha, ha, a few bragging rights. It's the *at least we did something right* song. I also can't forget the relationship that Paul shared with him. I remember peeking through the door as Paul knelt and prayed with him after a fun bedtime story with his best rendition of Ringo Starr as the conductor from Thomas the Tank Engine—it was sweet, and again, I am grateful for this.

Jordan had the best of two worlds, a daddy who fed him spiritually and a mommy who fed him his favorite – *Spinelli* and meatballs!

OWNING THE STATE OF NORMAL

Currently as in the movie "Groundhog Day," sometimes my days seem to repeat. I am fast forwarding to us currently. We are empty nesters now; I took on this endeavor to write my story because ever since it happened, people said that I need to tell this story. From a woman in the grocery store to a captive dinner party audience, 99% of people have said this. Write your story.

So, living in a new choice, and letting even the decision alone to change is *my new occupation*. What will I replace it with? I constantly tell myself, you have to remember and self-coach yourself, to realize and hope that you do not live there anymore. Let the past go. Something will live there in your "storage bank." Delete the old, bookmark this challenge, this new way of thinking.

You don't live there anymore! I heard that the other day, I heard that clearly, and it reminded me of an important lesson that I needed to hear over and over again. Sometimes every day, sometimes every minute. It was about that *day*, when I was given a new life, I was given a second chance! So, why do I go back to the past, when all I want to do is move forward? Why do I revisit those awful days and years? Perhaps they never left. Maybe they are still my pain, still my struggle, and I cannot avoid my reality. Maybe that's it, my reality is my nightmare—oh yeah.

My cell phone lies near me on my night table, and it usually wakes me up to remind me that I am going to have a great day or something happy like that. I have many apps of daily scriptures brightly popping up on my screen. There are also myriad positive-thinking messages, all flashing constantly across Facebook posts and amongst my 70,000 + emails. The message is great and hopeful—until my leg spasm jerks me out of bed, my feet hit the floor and I am quickly reminded to put my foot down firm, correctly, getting my other leg ready to move and function normally as my normal. My normal is not your normal. It's complicated because when my body was recovering from the paralysis, in the weakness, my stronger

121

working muscles compensated for the ones that weren't working anymore or working like they should be. And guess what, that weakness and strength dichotomy was just like my emotional state at the time. When I was weak, I did get stronger. In my weakness and sadness, I found hope. I am not playing with words. I was learning! I began to realize that when I was frustrated and weakened by all that, it led to hope, and that was a good thing. I needed to use hope to compensate for the challenging routine I faced every day. My rehab wasn't the usual 8-week prescription and then I recover to *as before.* This was long term, this was forever. I was already at what I felt was at the bottom, so the only place to go was up. It is time to shake off the dirt and get in a new game. I thought I would finally get to a place where I could say, "It is done. The hurt of remembering all the events of this pain. The past and all its trauma are there, but it still felt like there has to be a better choice of concentration that is liberating and transforming." I needed to forgive myself! I wish there were forgiveness pills, I would be taking those a lot. Maybe there are those pills, they are the ones so difficult to swallow. That's what bothered me, and it still does.

Forgive thyself is a spoonful of medicine that doesn't necessarily make your day more delightful or pleasant. To me, what it all came down to was that this was an accident. I did not plan to hurt myself, it happened, and I must move forward, try to forget the past and keep moving. I had to keep reminding myself that God in his love and mercy saved me when I did not even know him. His grace that day by stopping time and saving me and telling me to come back is all I need to concentrate on. That's a big statement to say but it's a bigger truth to live by. It takes faith and trust. Two virtues that kept frustrating me. I knew all about them, I just was afraid to walk on those waters for everything.

The effective way for me to process this was too realize that my memories are there *not* to torment me, but rather to *remind me* of all that I have *overcome.* The pressure to relive all the hurt and pain, and deal with many emotions again and again always get me back in the Groundhog Day movie mode. Those efforts that drive us to complete the story and start a new chapter in life, to move on, to begin anew, these efforts. It isn't easy. If you remember in the movie, Murray's' character kept stepping into the big puddle again and again. It took him awhile to see the flags before he eventually recognized them and stepped over and avoided that puddle. And especially avoided Ned Ryerson, the insurance salesman.

This really is for everyone going through a new plan of action. It is a daily effort. It is your plan, and when you get this message for yourself, you can begin. I can't remember where I heard this, but it was so inspiring to me: *"Learn to fall in love with the process!!"* A message of beginning. The *process* of new thinking, the process of getting up in the morning and focusing on a fresh start. The process of going to the gym, the process of learning about your body, the process of eating correctly, the process of getting up every day and starting again. It is a hard *new* to love. But it is you! No one, and I mean no one else can get your mind, body and spirit motivated enough to start. It must be you. Nike has made their famed tagline, "Just do it" stamped into our brains. Well then—just.

In the movie, Bill Murray's character desires to break the cycle of this new world that he is locked into, he is stuck in a twenty-four-hour revolving repeat of one awful day. But we really do not know how long he was actually stuck there in the world. Does he just resign to this or does he make lemonade out of his lemons? He falls in love and concurrently sheds himself of his own callous previous persona to enhance himself for his new love. He was changing, it was a process, but an important one. He began to get softer and began losing his old self for a better one. Every day in that world, he saved a boy falling from a tree, and he nurtured a homeless man and became his friend. He seemed to be at the right place at the right time, especially when he performed the Heimlich maneuver on a man and saved him from choking. Every new day he used the sameness, the repetitive loop, and he worked it to its advantages to learn a new language, master the piano, and compose poetry. But it was all because he fell in love with someone and took his eyes off himself just long enough to want that change. We see how much he changed when he cared for a homeless man and cried when he died. His change prepared him, when he did re-enter his old world, he would be extraordinary, and his love would find him to be compassionate, talented and lovable. Something his old self was not capable of being or doing.

So, self—how can I use my trauma, my *stuck in the same old attitude* to my advantage? Or, how can I overcome this and move on? Sometimes it feels like I'm a slow learner? Actually, quite the opposite, but when the first stumble of my toe hitting the ground happens, I am stuck, right back into defeat. I start the chants, my mental repeats of "I want to get out now—please give me a pardon, I have done my time, and I need to get out of jail." I scream this sometimes, it has been so long.

A lot of people tell me that I am an overcomer. They say that I have achieved so much, that I have done more than some people who do not have any mobility issues or any trauma such as I have. I sometimes see that person. That version of me has faded somewhat. The new version is another, not the courageous person as described. I've been asked the question of "How do I see myself?" Am I looking at the old Laurie, or the new one? Have I re-entered and reinvented myself in a better way, did I take advantage of my time and do something extraordinary? You can see the tennis match going on here.

When I look in the mirror, or when I think of my appearance what do I see and what is my opinion of myself? This seems to be a tricky question to ponder. As a woman, I have issues like any other woman. When we look in the mirror, we usually see all our faults. But as a woman who is also physically challenged or quadriplegic or God forbid, maybe say the term, "handicapped" when I look into the mirror, my reflection is always shocking. Not exaggerating here, it's just how it is. I can still see my

former self as I looked, for a mere second. It's sort of like the Phantom pain, an amputee might describe. The connection still feels like their limbs are still there. And sometimes they cannot embody the new device. The new artificial limb doesn't register in their brain as "belonging." I am like this too. This new body doesn't register as belonging to me either. My mind still thinks I am physically *able* or I look like I did. Maybe that's a good thing. The extended "getting used to" reflection, the new Laurie, that's the image I still must adjust to daily. I notice everything, my posture, my hands, my quirky spastic movements, they are my faults, this is what I see. Oh, to overcome this is more than to lose ten pounds, or do a juice-fast to reduce bloating, or get new highlights and then I'll feel better. Don't get me wrong, I love feeling skinny and getting a new "do," but as for my reflection, it's just still shocking, that's all I can say, that's just how it is. I am working through the process, I am seeing my straighter posture from working on the Pilates reformer. I am seeing a "not bad" for this body—not bad because I am still wearing clothes from twenty years ago, and still shopping in the "juniors" department—well sometimes. The emoji with the turned-up eyes fits so well here. Hey, don't laugh, it keeps me going.

"SUCH PATIENT LOVE"

If I were to write a love story, it would be titled "Such Patient Love," and it is the essence of my husband. This summer it will be thirty-one years that Paul and I are married. We vowed to each other our hearts and we've been so blessed. I'll share with you some of the beautiful card he wrote to me recently; it says so much about him, and our relationship.

> My love,
>
> We are entering the second chapter of our Love for each other, I am excited to see what's unfolding as we draw near to it. You have been climbing uphill in your battle to stay healthy and fit, you fight every day and you won't yield to defeat.
>
> That's inspiring! The small signs are showing, you will overcome, you will rise above, and You will be a Victor. Never stop improving your body mind and your spirit. That's the Girl I fell in love with. A Gentle Heart, a Tenacious Spirit and a Creative Mind.
>
> I love you, Laurie, and want nothing more than to spend the rest of my days with you. I believe in you, my Love, that every effort you put forth is like Sowing, you will reap.
>
> Let's trust the God who brought us together to keep us together for the next thirty years, the next decade, the next year, the next month, and this day. He is our Shepherd and He is with those who help us. We are with Him when we help others. Happy Anniversary, my Love, I love you.

How can I resist this kind of love? I have to give this man credit. He's in it with me until the end. Our years together have been an adventure. Ha, I don't think he realized what he was getting into. Neither did I. And he gives me his love, time and patience each and every day. Paul is my hidden treasure in all of this! The silver lining, the blessing, when that didn't ever seem possible. I used to wonder, especially after the fools I met before Paul—who would love me like this, love me how I am? My opinion of myself was small thinking. I entertained the circus of "No one will ever love you like this, you're too much to deal with. You can't do this, you can't do that"—the kind of self-hate talk that really didn't matter because it WASN'T TRUE! Thirty years later, we still love each other, in spite of all our obstacles and circumstances from the past and still in front of us. We put our faith hats on every day and remember that we've come a long way in rough waters and have survived.

HEY I'M STILL ME

I just watched the 2014 movie, "Still Alice." The character played by Julianne Moore has an early-age/advanced case of Alzheimer's disease. She was losing her memory quickly and the depiction is incredible. I identified with her so much, her "struggle" as she described, in a poignant speech late in the movie. She speaks about her Alzheimer's struggle. And the scary part for me is that, although her brain is the body part that is in decline, I relate to the loss, the significance of the shock, to see yourself change so much. She said, that she isn't Suffering, she is Struggling. *"Struggling to maintain who I once was!"* WOW! Could I relate to this!

Alice hoped with her doctor that her plateaus would keep her at a "good level." That she would be able to maintain this stage for a while. This would give her relief from the invisible powerful attack and change. Quickly, she was struggling, she was now on a daily track of losing, losing her mind and everything else that comes with a physical loss. The scene when she pees on herself was my life for a while. It feels like small, childlike behavior to be humbled like this is, it is so overwhelming, and I appreciated the perspective of her husband (Alec Baldwin). He gives her all the dignity she needs and deserves. He had life plans of his own that were put on hold. I liked his portrayal of loyalty. It is one of the largest ingredients in this bowl of dilemma and confusion, for the caretaker. She gets lost in her memories, her mind wanders through better days of her family from childhood. I'm drawn to old cherished memories myself. I longed to "have back" such precious years, good years that were safe. Anything before; that is "Before"—the cutoff in my timeline, that A-day.

One of my favorite scenes was when her youngest daughter finally is brave enough to ask a very changed mother how hard it is to adjust — "What does It feel like?"

Mom: "Not always the same, good days, bad days—on good days I could almost pass for a normal person, and on bad days—I feel like I can't find myself. I am defined by my intellect, my

129

language, my articulation, my inability to do so and I don't know who I am or what I'm going to lose next."

Daughter: "Sounds horrible."

Mom: "Thanks for asking."

What a rare but much needed conversation! So true. So sincere, it is good just to know when someone is "in it" with you. And that "in it" comes in all forms. From my experiences, people have a challenging time being involved in someone. Touching them physically is one thing but touching them in their souls is a gift few people have. I know, I am guilty myself, but it is necessary to touch people. Such a simple and obvious "elephant in the room" kind of thing. I mean we all have come face-to-face with an uncomfortable situation. Alice's daughter, who was getting frustrated with the "change" in her mother, took a necessary step. Instead of viewing her mom from afar, she put herself amidst her mother's pain. Sometimes the comfort of just knowing a true bond and assurance of love will keep that person going; in the long suffering when we become uniquely strengthened.

I can't count how many people in the last thirty-eight years—just about everyone, it's timeless—would excitedly say, "You need to write a book about yourself, it's unbelievable what you've experienced and look at you, etc., etc." Sometimes too much, primarily I figured, most people don't know how to respond to me when they hear some of the details. They really do not, so they either say, or like to say, something overtly pleasant without knowledge of just how obnoxious it sounds to me, or they are genuine. But, the number of people asking me to write a book has been long running. "BECAUSE SOMEONE WILL ALWAYS ASK" is a good alternate title for this story, because someone always will, and this is now okay for me. It's a big story and needs more than thirty seconds to convey what really happened—this will be year thirty-nine.

I say this a lot. I say I am still trying to *figure this out*. It happened, that's it, just move on now. Ahhhh, the brave soldier braving the storm: "Come on, get over your trauma already and join the rest of us, the really put-together people. You know, we who have never had anything so traumatic happen to us as you have but we've all dealt with hardships." I love this saying. Because it's only a pep talk, it's only a ten-second, "be positive" message. Oh Gosh—please, people! Do not say this to anyone who is dealing with something

130

beyond their control, when all has failed in body and spirit. When they cannot imagine the next few hours, let alone make lofty expectations for a better future of some sorts. My advice when you're faced with someone similar, in some despair of life, whatever it may be for them—touch and hold their hand, cry with them—leave the pep talk on the field.

HERE WE GO AGAIN!

All things become new, and they sure have. It has been ten years since we moved from sunny Florida when Paul got an opportunity to work at one of our nation's art museums in Washington, D.C. This was another new set of challenges, but we were getting used to this. At least this time we are closer to our family and friends in the New York area. This worked out well because we got a chance to reunite with them and see them more often. Our son had to deal with his own set of challenges in that it was his senior year of high school when we moved. A new state, a new city, and a new high school! I was proud of him. He registered for his classes that first day, and then he went to the football coach to see if he would take a new player on the team. He was the new kid on the block, but I guess he learned well. He did complain at first, but soon after making friends and settling in with a new high school crowd, he rolled with the new change. I told him, that at his age of eighteen, he should expect a lot of changes. It is supposed to be that way. You can learn a lot from new people and new ideas, but don't get stuck with your fingers getting hit by that lid on the box of frenemies. I had lots of experience with that, and it's just a waste of time. We need to put on our I CAN hats and make this work! I can proudly say that he took this challenge and came out shining. I am so proud that he did not let fear and anxiety, those two that I know so well, stop him from moving forward and taking this opportunity for what it could be. Besides, everyone back home was graduating and moving on anyway, right?

Living in the north again was something that I had to readjust to myself. And the very first winter, we had ice storms, a blizzard and a lot of time inside. I missed my house and pool in the backyard, and here the closest beach is over two hours away! I also had some funky accidents: I fell in the grocery store, we were rear-ended in the car, and I dislocated my shoulder playing Wii. My back and shoulder were now two issues on a steady basis to deal with and for which to seek physical therapy. We were trying to figure how I could get back into swimming and found a community with an indoor pool. Awesome, now I can continue my aqua routine even in winter months. However, I had started to feel numb and those symptoms were threatening. When this numbness traveled up into my arms and chest area, I then knew it wasn't from a heavy workout from the night before. Here we go again! Two weeks later, at a very prominent hospital, I was told as I sat on a hospital bed, that I needed spinal fusion surgery to decompress my neck at the C7 vertebra. This is what the numbness was from, and they also had to clean up another part of the C-4 area. A dreadful message on a dreadful day. Can this be coincidence again? Today was the *4th of September* 2013. Thirty-four years later, I was in a hospital and a doctor was telling me *again*, "We have to repair your neck!" SCREAM!

I did not like that doctor's report. I was admitted that evening, and I had every scan, MRI and other imaging they had available. *Just a side note: I had to convince the triage doctor that I needed to be seen because I was totally numb at that point. The medical community **still** is inept with spinal cord injuries because he thought I was faking this. He said that I shouldn't use an emergency room as a doctor's appointment. I seriously looked him in the eyes and said, "Look at that MRI and read it! Do you see the compression? I am numb! What am I supposed to do? Where am I supposed to go, back to my primary doctor?" I was later told by the doctors in "the back," behind those important double doors, that it was so good that I insisted to be seen. This is very serious! Ha, no kidding.

I searched for another opinion and I was so glad that we took the effort to do that. I highly recommend three opinions for such major surgery. I saw Doctor Brian Subach, president of the Virginia Spine Institute, well-known in this area for spine issues. We met his physician's assistant for about thirty minutes, and we went over my past history and these new symptoms. Meanwhile, the doctor was viewing the images I had brought and reading my charts. When he walked in, he came straight towards me with his arms open wide. A tall guy, with a bright smile and a fabulous tan. He hugged me! He said, "Wow, you've been doing this body for thirty-four years, and you're upright and your walking? Do you know how freaking hard this is?' He nodded at Paul. I smiled inside and outside, I hugged him back, he understood!

It always feels good when you meet someone who understands, especially a doctor. Again, you would think that this would just be common sense, but it's spinal cord, it's neuro, it's not known or understood even to all the "whitey" community. I had found my surgeon; this guy is going to do my neck! He pulled up the MRI and carefully and thoroughly described his procedure. He was confident and convincing in a good way that he could help me. A double surgery was scheduled, and he did the posterior (back of neck) repair, and he decompressed a spur at C7. He put six screws into my neck bones to strengthen that area. Two days later he did the anterior, in the front of the neck, and he installed two titanium plates to secure. I laughed when they gave me a card with the skeletal image of my hardware in my neck. Just in case I have to explain to TSA at the airport.

The surgery was successful, and a few months later I was swimming again! It is major rehab time again! I was in for another fight, and this time I am not eighteen, but in my early fifties. A big difference for anyone, a huge difference for me. Here we go again. I had to adjust to the rehab that was planned. As I searched, I wanted to find a therapist I could work with and I needed some major attention. I was strong in my workout endeavors, but really, this felt like a truck ran me over backwards and then in the front. This was going to take a while, and like I said, I am older now. This is round two, baby, well, not really, but I need to prepare, for the mind and the body. Again.

I found a new physical therapy clinic, and a new physical therapist at Restore PT & Wellness. They highlighted wellness using traditional physical therapy and also offered Pilates, yoga and massage therapy. I always knew about Pilates but never tried it because I couldn't imagine doing all that breathing and just gliding on that *thing,* the Reformer, it seemed too simple. I mean you're just gliding back and forth on that machine. Ha ha, the reality is that it will kick your hiney, and it will transform your bod!

Well, to my delight, I found a physical therapist, Viraj, who is also a certified Pilates instructor, and we began my new love. I soon found out that I did not know how to breathe correctly, so we worked on that for a few weeks. It was going to be a "let's see how you do" approach because this new therapist hardly knew me and did not know my base line. She did not know what was *normal* for me. Well, I'm glad to say, we figured it out and now a few years post-surgery, I am doing a thirty- to forty-minute routine on my own Reformer and I'm loving it! The exciting news is that there have also been changes in this body. This thirty-eight-year-old, spinal cord injured body chooses involuntarily to still frustrate me and cause physical and emotional bursts of pain. I am proud to say that I have had some major improvements. My bowel issues have been restored to a once-a-day deposit. And through Pilates, my forever sleeping abdominals have come alive! I found my TA's, *a difficult achievement for anyone*, Viraj said! Don't ask me how or why, but it is the first time in all these years that I can honestly say that I feel a contraction and can feel muscles in that area again! Oh yeah, this quad has abs! Ha, they are in process and nothing like what we see all over social media, but they are starting, and I am doing whatever it takes to get results. So far, I can see some indents on the tummy, and I look forward to lifting my shirt to show them off! This quad does Pilates!

V.C. — HER THOUGHTS

I have been fortunate enough to walk alongside Laurie on her physical fitness journey over the course of three years. Throughout this journey, I have played the role of physical therapist, Pilates instructor and most importantly, companion. Even though I am a seasoned PT and Pilates instructor, Laurie's everyday life is something I had never encountered, and to say that it has been an eye-opening experience is an understatement. Routine tasks, such as rolling over in bed, sitting up, standing, walking short distances and even taking a bath are all tasks that she has mastered, but they initially presented a significant challenge in Laurie's day-to-day life. For a recovering spinal cord injury patient, those innate tasks require significantly more mental and physical exertion than the average individual. A simple visit to physical therapy in the morning may deplete Laurie of any reserves she might have for the remainder of the day.

Through it all, Laurie has met her challenges head-on in her fearless, undaunting, and frankly inspiring manner. Step by step and day by day, she manages the aches and pain she wakes to with fitness. Instead of viewing them as hindrances, Laurie views these opportunities to stretch, strengthen, and regain balance within her body. She packs her bag for a swim. She gets geared up and ready for Pilates on the Reformer. She does not hesitate to make the most of a beautiful day, and she inspires herself for an outdoor recumbent bike ride. Her mind awakens her body. There is a constant struggle/conversation between her brain and her muscles. Her brain inevitably wins.

I had not learned the details of the event that led to Laurie's injury until recently. I met Laurie when she came to

137

physical therapy after new complications in her cervical spine, which ultimately required surgery. She had to have surgery near the level of her original injury and was clearly anxious about getting treatment at all. It did not take long for me to learn that she was motivated, mentally strong and goal-oriented with unbelievable drive. She wanted to get back to one of her favorite pastimes of swimming. We got her to her goal, back into the pool, and she graduated to physical therapy. A few years went by and she was back with a knee injury. That provided a window of opportunity to master a new passion, Pilates. I began instructing her the foundations of Pilates – breathing and how to engage her absent core. Now that Laurie had regained control of her mind and body, she had specific fitness goals in mind. It was incredible when I heard that she had found Pilates to "turn on" certain muscles that had been dormant. The exercises have helped her gain precision in her gait and balance. She also discovered how Pilates can stretch, lengthen and decompress her spine to aid in pain relief. The reformer supports her spine and helps her to stabilize and access the muscles that were otherwise inaccessible. She has even started performing Pilates in her swim sessions at the pool, and we have termed this "Aqualates," patent pending.

I am utterly amazed at Laurie and her recent transformation. Her mental and physical achievements are inspiring to all who are witness to it. Her drive in reaching her health and wellness goals has been exemplary. My time with Laurie has bettered me not only as a health provider but personally as well. Laurie has demonstrated that no matter how unsurmountable an obstacle may be, a positive outlook and drive can overcome almost any shortcoming. There's nothing a little zap can't cure!

Viraj Chang MPT/CPI

LEARNING AS WE GO...

I have mentioned before the topic of movement, especially the lack of it. In the Spinal Cord Injury world, the obsession with a bowel and bladder routine is essential. It's the hidden part of the injury. Even though, to most people, the obvious topic of movement lies in whether or not you can move an arm, finger, leg or toe. It is the function of your exiting; did you or could you move your bowels, and can you pee, urinate, or void. I was very fortunate to have a bladder that was willing to cooperate with the program at the time. I had knowledge that my bladder was able to work on command. I did have many accidents and struggled with the retraining of urinary rehab. Unfortunately, it is a trial and error sort of thing, but in essence if you are blessed to be doing this type of training your well ahead of the game, especially for a C-6 injury. How the body functions, are linked to the level of your spine, the spinal cord segments serve specific motor and sensory regions of the body, i.e., breathing, arm sensation, leg sensation, sensory awareness, organ function. Doctors will always refer to how those functions are affected from your injury.

My bottom half did not answer the "return" call so quickly. Twenty years of S&E, those are, suppositories and enemas. In fact, at year twenty, I found some help that came with a unique promise. We vacationed at an Orlando hotel that year. And as you may know, the staff usually wear name plates from their hometowns or country. So, as our server, "Jose from Columbia," suggested to my brother, who was having a "hard" time while on vacation, he brought him a box of All-Bran cereal. Jose said, "Senior, I guaranteeeee—," and that became a favorite new expression and private joke for us in my family. Five minutes later, my brother wasn't exactly looking for el baño, he was running. I was so jealous. Anyone with these issues can attest. In only five minutes or less, relief was on its way for him. We left that day to go home and stopped by the supermarket to get the exact cereal that helped his troubles. It took my body seven days to get relief, but it did work! This was a miracle—on my own, without any of my previous and necessary friends, S&E. This quad can poop!

Fast forward to these current years, I mentioned before that I believe that my determination to improve this body in whatever way possible, would also take a lot of discipline and a share of testing. What would help me was deliberately related to exercise, nutrition and much needed support. I had two out of three of these ingredients, and recently the combination is working.

After my recent spinal fusion in 2013, I began to step up the process. I continued swimming to do the initial rehab because it was less stress and would prepare me for anything harder. I also integrated Pilates, free weights, mat work, and recumbent bike riding. I also committed to a new way of eating and joined the "clean" approach. Together, Paul and I began to reduce certain foods out of our diet. We stopped eating sugar, flours, and reduced the amount of red meat. We increased vegetables, and substitute flours for grains and also stay away from the ominous gluten. I don't think we have a problem with gluten, but it makes us feel better and actually enjoy the search for the replacements. Daunting as it may seem to some, it really is possible. And the big news for me is that, with the change in eating, I now can find relief every day...I am amazed at this. It was always a difficult topic and often frustrated me to tears. I believe that due to the good eating now, my body is showing signs that it does make a difference. And the combination with my workouts, has strengthened my pelvic floor in this area for the success. The breathing technique involved with *breath in* and *breathe out*, takes a lot of control and concentration for me. The brain-to-body part signal sometimes works, and sometimes it gets overloaded.

I am grateful for the relentless coaching and encouragement from my P.T. who is now familiar with my consuming questions and curiosity. I think that my forever hope in finding out how to improve and function better is also the key. In this area of concentration, I won't quit the routine and hopefully the routine won't stop working. This quad poops every day!

I NEVER SLOWED DOWN LONG ENOUGH TO QUIT!

Continuing with my rehab, routine, exercise, workout, or whatever you want to call it…it is working!

I have bigger dents! That's what I call the higher Rectus abdominal muscles that are just beginning to get defined but trust me I have a long way to go. I've always been curious if Quadriplegics can get a six pack or not. I mean is it, physically possible to firstly, feel your abdominals, and then get to that six pack level ? There isn't a lot of reading material on that.

Currently, I am seeing improvements because I am loving the process of creating a new me!! *I need another year*! That is my current phrase for my long-term goals; that is, longer than a week! I have a routine of free weights, mat work and stretching. I try to balance my workouts with swimming as well. The water is great for its buoyancy and allows me to run, jump and do aerobics. In the pool I do an aqua workout that, I would challenge anyone, able bodied or not, to try. I might be riding my recumbent bike in the next 5K race that Virginia Spine will host next October! Body permitting, that is. I still need to be careful and not overload my body. Must be age, my body is warning me more often, to slow down.

The usually annoying and difficult DOMS- delayed onset muscle soreness for me usually results in a more permanent time period, hence my nickname POMS. Recently, I even attempted rowing. I met with the adaptive rowing program, which has spinal cord and special needs people who love to be athletic and competitive. I loved meeting these athletes, people with incredible physical loss, there they are rowing for an hour, maybe two. They certainly inspired me to try, rowing is kick your butt hard. I can certainly do the strap-in method, where they strap your lower body, hip, core and upper chest; and you basically row with all back, chest and arm muscles. But me being me, no, I wanted to do the *normal* or traditional stroke, so I'll train and lay off that for now

141

and wait until next year. I have to think this way now, I have to choose my battles, so to speak. Preservation over impulsiveness. My body appreciates this now. I love thinking new.

My P.T. just asked me, during one of my latest rehabs, "why do you have to work out every day? You need rest, slow down." I replied without hesitation, " this is what I do, I work out." It seemed odd after I thought about it. It really is all I do. My day is designed about wellness and its efforts or to at least try!

It's difficult to maintain a winning positive attitude. But I try my best. I get by with a little help from my family and friends. Recently, my brother Richie, shared with me his sincere feelings about what happened to me, his little sister. He called me his *hero*, because of my ability to face my challenges and still smile and be able to find ways to improve in my difficult circumstances. We cried because our family has had so many obstacles to overcome; and we have. We stayed connected even though we didn't at times, we always held onto hope, that treasure, which says in the face of adversity, we can overcome. So true. It's an understatement but a trueness. It's real, meaning, the help from your family and friends; it is what helps you get by. I am referring to letting people help you. You need to let those surrounding you figure out solutions for your well-being. I could remember thinking, that I had to be the only one to figure it all out now. Other people didn't know. They didn't know what I was going through. True, they don't , but they can try if you let them. I'm also referring to letting it play out without all the grunting and crying and seeing the bigger picture. Their help, their kindness is a gift and blessing. And they come in all shapes and sizes. Try not to live isolated in your misery. Try to make an effort. That's the getting by part and it's a softer road to travel. We all are on roads; some very rocky, some with gravel and are messy. Some are smoothed out and paved. It's a long road and the mile marker gets blurry sometimes. But it's a long road with many important stops to make.

OH, THE THINGS PEOPLE SAY!

"I've got my eye on you!" She yelled loudly to overcome the bad acoustics as I entered the indoor pool. "I think you are one classy bitch on that scooter!" I hesitated for a moment but continued as planned, to do my aqua workout before my writers meeting. She was referring to my electric scooter, it is like a Segway, but it has three wheels and it is the coolest. She was doing her own thing in the three-foot section of the pool, and once more she continued with her thoughts. "You are so cool and look fabulous on that thing, so I figure when I am ready for one of those, I'll get in touch with you." I tried not to giggle too much, but "when she is ready"? That's the line that got me, her silver hair already told me how old she might be. I turned to her and thanked her for her compliments and swam away thinking, "Did I just get a compliment?" Mine are so unusual. I must be getting thicker skin because that whole conversation would have destroyed me when I was younger. I laughed again, thinking I should start a company with that name, Classy Bitch Inc., or a nonprofit for women to stop name-calling. When things like these happen, I often borrow the only and suitable phrase: "You can't make this stuff up." These conversations must have a meaning, maybe they should be told. There always seems to be a message to me. Mostly, I sense that people who say the oddest things are like a red flag waving in my face, a guide, saying, "Come back to the truth. Put this all-in perspective and keep doing your thing."

Through the years, I've been called a few odd names, mostly because people get nervous when you are different. They may want to think, that they are being gracious or assume that referring to you as one of the more proper terms such as "handicapped" or "disabled" is okay. Then they are justified in being politically correct. I am being sarcastic now, if you don't already know. And then, just when I have had my fill of beating myself up and vowing that the next time I meet someone who says the "wrong" thing to me, that person is going to get my full rage. Oh, the next time!

After a rough morning; sometimes I get the feeling that all *this* is useless. *This* as in my efforts to improve my body, and all my efforts to "get better." It's that familiar routine song of depression generating a melody of *I am stuck* like this, why bother? I find myself weary in my efforts today, but I have been here before, and I have heard that song all too many times. I push myself to a morning swim. I walk into the locker room, which can be a challenge without the scooter because I must carry my heavy bag of clothes and change of clothing, swim shoes, towels, etc. A challenging *balance act* to walk and carry at the same time. I enter the locker room, struggling to get to the changing area, and a woman says to me," It's rough to get here, especially on a cold rainy day as this." Disturbed that I had to now converse, walk and carry my bag, I muffled back to her, "Rough? Yeah, it is." She added, "Are you at least progressing?" In my usual sarcastic tone, I replied, "Thirty-eight years of progress. I broke my neck when I was eighteen, was quadriplegic, got a miracle and walk again—yeah, I'm progressing." Her hesitation was familiar because I guess you don't meet people every day who break their neck and walk again! Especially in a gym locker room. She said, "Wow, that is a huge miracle, I am so happy for you!" I was waiting…*one, two, three*-boom, there it is! She joined all those people who quickly replied, "You should write a book." I thanked her and sat in the changing room, once again torn between crying and remembering I really did get a miracle. "Why are you so depressed, suck it up and get to your workout! You don't have time to cry."

I also remembered what someone else said to me. Before I began writing this book, I met a woman named Ruth. One evening on our way out; after visiting my husband's parents in their assisted living facility, we heard a woman's voice. Ruth had a stroke a year ago and barely spoke—except to me. As I passed her, she was sitting in the lobby, hunched over in her wheelchair. Her eyes were watching the front door and watching the everyday usual's. She may have been waiting for a visit as she glanced at the door with a hopeful eye, or she may have just wanted to be "out." Out from her room and the same old routine. Her voice grew loud as she boldly sat up and raised her chest upwards to purposely look at me and said, "You can do it—you can." She smiled, and she fell back into her low posture. She was quiet and gazed. "So odd," the desk attendant said, "she hardly speaks anymore and when she does it's only for necessary things."

My husband was with me, and we both thought, "Wow!" "Yeah great," I actually thought. Now I have another *message, but* from whom? It must mean something, I always get messages in strange ways. But what—what is the thing *I can do?* Was it this book, was it something else? Or was the message for the everyday grind, that I can do this life—*I can still do "it."*

Some have also called me a light. A broken vessel, some have referred to this allegory, that although not perfect or complete, *she lets that work for her.* (Yes, it was said.) "Laurie, let your light shine, let your heart be soft. Let yourself be teachable and do all that you can do to keep it soft." I love the contrast of broken and used. Incomplete and determined. There is a purpose for everything, sometimes it may take a while to see the message.

Not everyone gets noticed for remarkable things, great beauty or accolades of valor—some of us get noticed because we are different, it's odd to explain, this "admiration" of some. And that's okay, because everyone has a story, and some have stories to be told. I have gotten a lot of mixed messages through the telling of mine. It is not the life story I would have written. I would have loved another story so totally different. But in all that search for those big questions of why and how come, there is the unending conversation. It always comes back to the unchanged reaction. Beware, if you do. I usually have an answer ready and share my struggle with a humorous version of my pain. But mostly hope! It is a large story I think, I mean that I cannot leave out major details. And this usually means that I will mention my belief in Jesus. Faith is an essential element in my life. Hope in God; to *hope* in times of hopelessness. I hope against all odds. I hope in His *grace* that has brought me this far. I do not have seven steps to a better life. I do not have a formula for $14.99, and if you call me now, you can have two books or CDs. I have my story, my determination, my pain, my forbearance, even my joy, but it is real. It is this life. A constant mix of joy, grief and sometime clueless long seasons. Oh my. I sound so grown up now. I intentionally choose every day to be hopeful. From our miraculous births to being sustained in our elder years, we all can see how faith and hope and love have kept people *well* and thriving in their mind, body and spirit. Isn't this what we all want? To live peaceably and positive.

To end our lives with purpose and meaning—and we hope it will be with a smile on our face. Hope triggers the mind to keep purpose, hope triggers the body to keep going. My hope is in who first loved me. He saved me in the pool and saved me for eternity. He has kept me alive and has brought me back. Incomplete? Maybe, but complete enough to let his light shine through my darkness to tell my story. What or whom do you put your hope in?

THE 4th OF SEPTEMBER:
WHAT IS IT ABOUT THAT DAY?

Every first weekend of September, we all have a reminder that summer is ending, and a new season will begin. I usually try to avoid making plans for that upcoming holiday weekend that most of us celebrate with a long beach weekend and a burger by the grill. A hurry to get in the last bit of sun and sand type of activity. School is just beginning, and moms are running around stores getting No.2 pencils or anything else on that teachers list.

My weekend activities included duck and hiding. I usually hide and try to avoid the celebration festivities. I don't need to stir up those tapes that are just dying to be released in my head. Replays of that weekend and highlights of the moment in the pool.

Last year, I got up, with a new attitude. I intended to make this a great day. I decided to do the opposite, I didn't want to give any play to those old dramas. I made chocolate chip raspberry pancakes and packed our swim bags.

I decided we weren't going to stay home and sulk and even entertain any previews of any type. Even the grateful memories. I'm putting on my swimsuit, getting ready to do the opposite of what I usually did.

It was going to commence a great day with new memories and a new tradition.

. However, this Labor Day weekend we had another version of September 4th. Paul was cleaning some leaves off the patio and suddenly stood up holding his chest. He went inside to cool off, and was pacing back and forth, until he banged on the door for me to call 911. They arrived quickly, and I saw my husband; he is strong, muscular and "looking good for his age." That's what everyone says when you've past a certain age, and your belly is lean, *your beating the odds*. Well, he's that guy who follows the program. He works out five days a week, eats clean and is down to a good weight. He's hitting goals and I even got him doing Pilates, yes, real men do Pilates! He loves the reformer work and it shows.

So, what the heck? What happened just now? ... because when I saw the emergency tech put in an IV and ask for the nitro, I got dressed and off we went to the hospital.

He had a heart attack and was admitted for a stent procedure. We were in shock! How could this happen to a guy who takes care of himself and watches everything he eats. He doesn't fit the profile the doctor said. They said stress must have induced this, stress perhaps from work. In this region that's the type of heart attack they see. It's not the tobacco belt (smokers) or bread belt (high cholesterol) types found in other areas.

"You survived the widowmaker, sir.," the cardiac surgeon said. Again, "patients like you aren't the norm, but you are now a cardiac patient for life. And on the meds for life." Wow our faces showed our shock and he quickly added, you're lucky, you probably survived due to how well you've taken care of yourself.

Lucky.

Paul came home two days later. Now what? How long does he stay home? Can he go back to work? There is stress there. Again. All these questions. Bigtime health issues. Life and death. All this again.

We went to bed exhausted, we held each other and cried. We both said, "what just happened." And it happened on that day, on that weekend. The one we were enjoying and also nicely avoiding, my A-day. Trying to put a positive twist on it. Trying to be happy. "On this day? You get a heart attack? This is too crazy." I was complaining, I can't comprehend that on Sept. 4th *again*, we were in need of major help, miraculous help. I texted friends to pray for him, and I complained in my texts as well. My friend Katie, replied, "think of it like this, now every September 4th, it is no longer a day of hurt and pain, but now a day of celebration, because Paul survived, it is the day that God saved Paul!"

Like I said, "What a day!"

"For now, we see but a faint reflection of the riddles and mysteries as though reflected by a mirror, but one day we will see face to face. My understanding is *incomplete* now, but one day I will understand everything, just as everything about me has been fully understood.

Until then, there are three things that remain, faith, hope and love---yet love surpasses them all. So above all else, let love be the beautiful prize for which you run."

1 Corinthians 13: 12-13

THE END-MAYBE

41936590R00097

Made in the USA
Middletown, DE
11 April 2019